A Short History of Chicago

For Alice Hamilton Cromie,
who was discovered in
Independence, Missouri.

A Short History of Chicago

Robert Cromie

LEXIKOS

San Francisco

First published in September 1984 by
LEXIKOS
1012 14th Street
San Francisco, California 94114

Edited by Abby Levine
Designed by CABA
Production by Carlton Herrick/QR, Inc.
Text set in Stempel Palatino
Printed and bound by Edwards Bros.

Library of Congress Cataloging in
Publication Data

Cromie, Robert.
    A short history of Chicago.

      Bibliography: p.
      Includes index.
      1. Chicago (Ill.)—History.   I. Title.
F548.3.C79 1984 977.3'11 82-49334
ISBN 0-938530-28-3

84 85 86 87 5 4 3 2 1

Contents

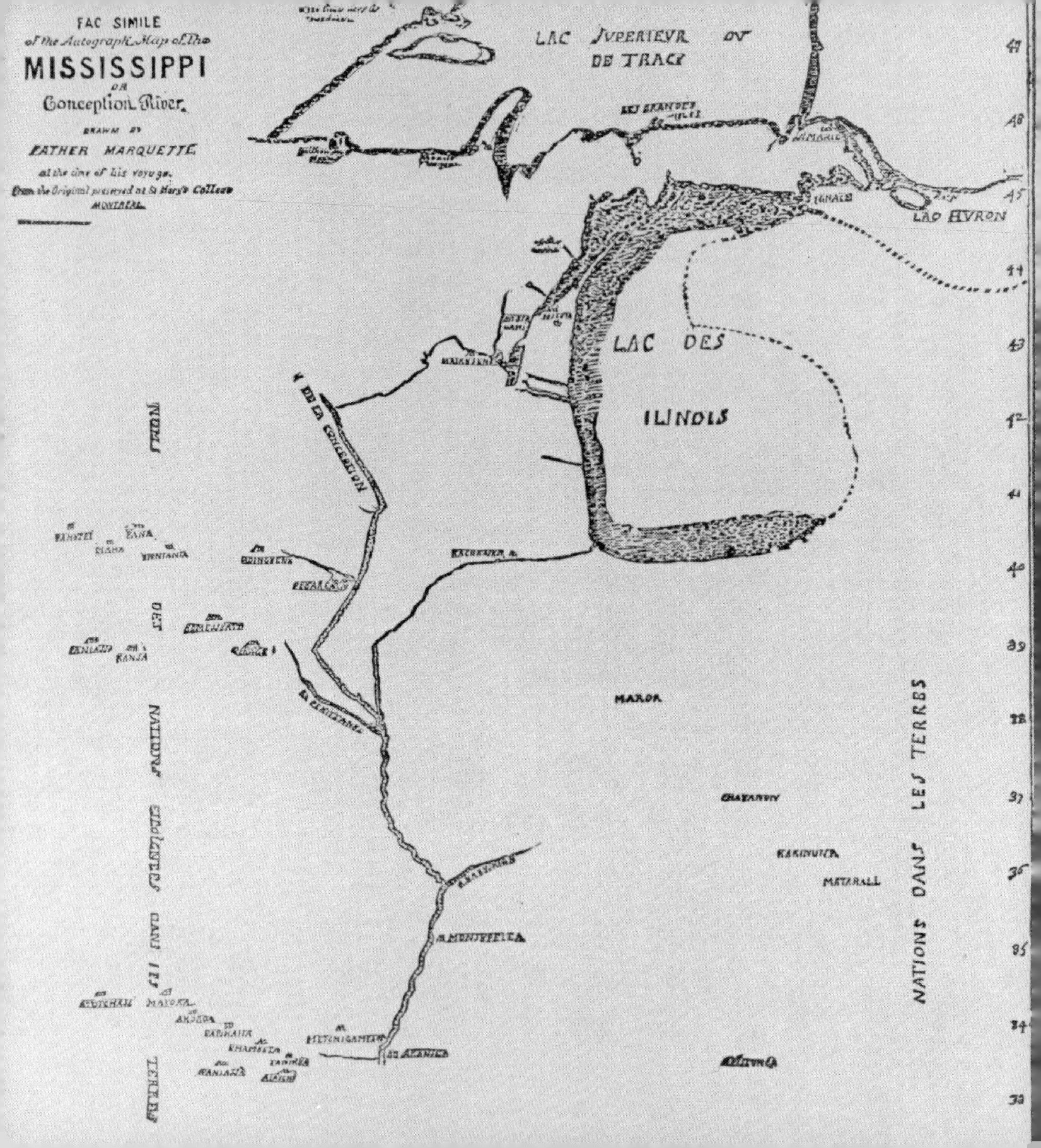

FAC SIMILE
of the Autograph Map of the
MISSISSIPPI
OR
Conception River.

DRAWN BY
FATHER MARQUETTE
at the time of his voyage
from the Original preserved at St Mary's College
MONTREAL

LAC SVPERIEVR OV
DE TRACE

47

48

LES GRANDES
ISLES

S.MARIE

45

LAC HVRON

IGNACE

44

LAC DES

43

ILINDIS

42

MISKONSING

MASKOVTENS

41

R. DE LA CONCEPTION

40

KACHKAKVA R.

MAROA

39

38

CHAVANON

37

KAKINONBA

36

METABALL

35

KABAYKIA

34

MONFPERLA

NATIONS DANS LES TERRES

33

METCHIGAMEA

AKANSEA

The Lonely Beginnings

1

During the winter of 1833–34, "on a fine moonlit night, when the ice was good, the whole of Chicago turned out for a skate and a frolic, and we had it. There must have been at least a hundred persons on the river between Wells Street and the Forks."

We can never know who planned this moonlit caper, later remembered by Charles Cleaver, who had arrived earlier that year from London with his guns and "some good-bred dogs." Did Mark Beaubien, the jolly host of the Sauganash Hotel, play his famous fiddle as he glided along? Did any of the Fort Dearborn garrison join in the fun? Were there Indians among the merrymakers or watching from the banks? Did everyone gather at one of the few houses in town when the air grew too nippy to continue the gala? And it would be very satisfying to know whether that young lady was present who, when she became an old lady, wistfully remarked that "the early settlers in Chicago were among the happiest people in the world."

That faraway night with everyone whirling over the ice would be a delightful jumping-off place for our short history of a great city. But it was more than half a century after the arrival in the area of Jean Baptiste Point du Sable, who for a long time *was* Chicago. Du Sable in turn was preceded by the many Frenchmen who passed through or paused in the region during the 17th and 18th centuries. And, of course, before everyone were the Indians—Illinois, Miamis, Weas, and Pottawatomies—who gave the area its name.

It was the Chicago Portage that attracted these visitors. This narrow watershed connected Lake Michigan by way of the Chicago River with the Desplaines River and thence the Illinois and Mississippi. The portage was both a natural meeting place and the gateway through which travelers

The word "Che-cau-gou," first written in 1680 in an account of La Salle's expedition, was given at various times to the Illinois, Desplaines and Chicago Rivers (it also seems to have been the name of a line of Indian chiefs). The original meaning perhaps was "great," and it may have additionally meant "skunk cabbage," "wild onion," or garlic."

Opposite page
Marquette's Terra Incognita: Lac des Illinois is now Lake Michigan. After that, you're on your own.

Before wake-up time: The Indians, a few wandering traders, and Jean Baptiste du Sable knew where Chicago was—or wasn't—late in the 18th century.

passed on their way north or south. Some of these wanderers had definite missions; other were restless-footed, curious about what lay across the prairie or eager to follow a river and see where it led. The tribes used the portage during hunting trips, when war parties were passing through, or for councils. And because Chicago was on a route much used by the Indians, traders came to set up posts, and missionaries and the early French explorers arrived, remained for a time, and eventually moved on.

The Chicago area was low and swampy, without many trees. But the seemingly endless prairie was close at hand. And thanks to recurrent visits over the centuries of glaciers grinding down from the northland, the Illinois region possessed not only a variety of lakes, including the magnificent Illinois (later called Lake Michigan), but a varied and useful assortment of rivers, large and small. The fabled Mississippi, which everyone talked about but few (other than Indians or an occasional *coureur de bois* seeking furs) ever saw before the beginning of the eighteenth century, lay somewhere to the west. Many believed it emptied into the Pacific Ocean.

The best known of the early travelers were the team of Père Jacques Marquette and Louis Jolliet, and the dashing if sometimes difficult René-Robert Cavelier, sieur de La Salle, who went all the way to Texas in quest of a new empire for his king, Louis XIV—as well as some choice land grants for himself.

A Short History of Chicago

French Exploration: In 1672 officials of New France (Canada) asked Jolliet to follow the Mississippi to its ultimate destination. With the missionary Marquette and five *voyageurs*, the intrepid Frenchman left St. Ignace, near Mackinac, in May 1673. They crossed Wisconsin to the Mississippi and followed that unknown river south until July 17, when their canoes were near the mouth of the Arkansas. Then, fearful of encountering hostile Spaniards, the tiny expedition turned north again, having determined that the great river ran into the Gulf of Mexico and not the Pacific Ocean.

Père Jacques Marquette: In 1673, he ventured down the Mississippi as far as the Arkansas; he died in 1675 en route from Chicago to his home mission.

Weary of battling the Mississippi current, they instead paddled up the Illinois and stopped at the village of Kaskaskia (near what is now Utica). Here the Indians were so taken with Marquette that one of the chiefs and a party of braves escorted their visitors over the Chicago Portage to the Lake of the Illinois, as Lake Michigan was then known.

The group reached the Jesuit mission at Green Bay, Wisconsin, before stopping for the winter, but as soon as the ice had vanished in the spring of 1684, Jolliet began the final leg of his journey. His boat overturned, however, only a short distance from Quebec, and Jolliet's papers and journal were lost, as well as "the little slave, ten years old, who had been presented to me. He was endowed with a good disposition, full of talent, diligent and obedient; he made himself understood in French and began to read and write." Jolliet never returned to what became Chicago.

Ill much of that summer, Marquette at last returned to Kaskaskia in accordance with his promise to the Indians. He left with a small party on October 25, 1684, but when winter caught him at the Chicago Portage, he had to spend the ice-bound months in a cramped cabin owned by two French traders. One account of his last journey declares that with spring, Marquette went on to Kaskaskia and said Mass there on Easter Sunday. Another version maintains that he was too ill to continue and instead began the homeward journey along the eastern shore of the lake as soon as the weather had moderated. Both stories agree that the gentle priest died on May 18, 1675, near the site of what is now Ludington, Michigan.

Jolliet was forced to recreate his account of the trip from memory, but luckily Marquette's records remained intact. The city of Joliet, Illinois, is named in the explorer's honor. Father Marquette is remembered by Marquette, Michigan, and the Père Marquette Railroad.

Another sometime French visitor to the Chicago Portage was La Salle. With the aid of his friend, Henri de Tonty (called Tonty of the Iron Hand because of a battle injury in Sicily), he supervised the building of several forts, among them Crèvecoeur near Peoria and St. Louis at Starved Rock. After a series of misadventures including the loss of his cargo-rich vessel, the *Griffon* (first to sail the Great Lakes) and Tonty's capture by Indians, La Salle and Tonty did reach the mouth of the Mississippi. There, on April 9, 1682, La Salle claimed for Louis XIV all the land touched by the Mississippi or its tributaries. He named this casually acquired kingdom Louisiana.

For God, King, and Country: La Salle claims the great river and all its watershed.

Back in Canada, La Salle found that a new governor and old rivals had cost him two of his trading posts. He sailed immediately for France, where his posts were restored and he was named governor of Louisiana. Unfortunately, the Sun King also directed La Salle to set sail from France for the mouth of the Mississippi, there to found a French colony. The fleet of four ships, with 400 men, was delayed by La Salle's illness in the West Indies and by Spaniards who captured the supply ship. Their number soon dwindled to 180 and, although they reached the Gulf of Mexico, no one aboard could find the Mississippi. La Salle and his weary men landed at Matagorda Bay, close to what is now Galveston, either late in 1684 or early the next year.

A Short History of Chicago

Nothing went well. After many bitter months, during which overland scouts failed to locate the big river, La Salle and about half of the remaining 45 colonists, short of supplies, sick, and hungry, departed for Illinois to find Tonty. That was in January 1687. Some two months later, perhaps not yet out of Texas, La Salle was murdered by one of his own people.

Only a handful of the ragged colonists reached Illinois. Tonty, who already had led one search for La Salle, was told of his friend's fate. He gallantly again set off to find the body of the great explorer. He had no success, and died in Louisiana in 1700.

Ironically, none of these early visitors to the muddy Chicago Portage could see anything particularly promising in this area through which they passed en route to somewhere else. No one dreamed that one of the world's great cities was to have its beginnings there less than a century later.

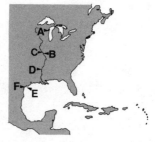

A. Green Bay
B. Mississippi River
C. Kaskaskia
D. Mouth of Arkansas
E. Matagorda Bay
F. Galveston

From Nowhere to Nothing

2

The early decades of the 18th century found much of the territory near Chicago in turmoil. The Indian tribes were on the warpath, both against each other and the advancing white trappers and explorers. It was extremely dangerous to use the Chicago Portage. In 1700 the French priests Pierre François Pinet and Julian Bineteau closed the Mission of the Guardian Angel of Chicago, which had been founded in 1696. The two men went to more tranquil surroundings. According to A. T. Andreas, the author in 1886 of a superb three-volume *History of Chicago*, "For more than half a century, the name Chicago is not mentioned, and there is no record of any visit by a white man to the locality."

The situation changed rapidly as the century drew to a close. One factor was the 1763 Treaty of Paris, by which the French surrendered Canada and the American Midwest to the English. Another was the formation of the Northwest Territory by the United States Congress in 1787, four years after the official end of the War of the American Revolution.

The creation of the Northwest Territory opened public lands for sale in a huge area later to become the states of Ohio, Illinois, Indiana, Michigan, Wisconsin, and part of Minnesota. When the Northwest Territory was established, its inhabitants included an estimated 25,000 Indians and 2,000 Frenchmen. Although the first American settlement was at Marietta, Ohio, in April 1788, British claims to parts of the Territory were not ended until the War of 1812.

Upset by the number of settlers streaming into the alluring Northwest Territory, the Indians were becoming increasingly hostile. After numerous whites were slain or made captive, President George Washington sent one of

Opposite page
Precarious foothold: The first Fort Dearborn in 1803.

his finest military men, Gen. "Mad Anthony" Wayne, into Ohio in 1792 to deal with the threat. Wayne did so in 1794 by defeating a large band of Indians near the Maumee River (southwest of what is now Toledo) in the Battle of Fallen Timbers. In the Treaty of Greenville that followed—one of the first of many forced Indian cessions of land to the United States—the Indians gave up land for three forts, including "one piece of Land Six Miles Square at the mouth of the Chickago River emptying into the Southwest end of Lake Michigan where a fort formerly stood."

In 1796 the British officially yielded all of their posts in the Northwest Territory to their former colony. And in 1803 the United States bought the Louisiana Territory from France for $15 million. This was one of the shrewdest real estate deals of all time since the total area acquired—about 828,000 square miles—doubled the territory of the new nation.

The Man from Santo Domingo: The earliest public reference to Jean Baptiste Point du Sable—Chicago's first permanent resident—seems to have been in 1799, when Col. Arent Schuyler DePeyster, British commander at Mackinac, mentioned "Baptiste Point DeSaible, a handsome Negro, well educated and settled at Eschikagou but much in the French interest." Later that same year, du Sable, a prosperous trader, was arrested on suspicion of spying against the British by Lt. Thomas Bennett of the King's Regiment near the present Michigan City, Indiana. He was taken to Mackinac where, according to Bennett, "since his imprisonment he has in every respect behaved in a manner becoming to a man in his situation, and has many friends who give him a good character."

The sequence of du Sable's movements now becomes untraceable, but he must have returned to Chicago within a reasonably short time. In 1790, a Detroiter, Hugh Heward, came through the area and stopped for provisions at du Sable's place (near the present site of the *Chicago Sun-Times* building). He was provided with flour, bread, and pork. This means, as the late Very Reverend Thomas A. Meehan points out, that du Sable must have had his own flour mill, hogs, crops, and even baker. Writing in the *Journal of the Illinois Historical Society*, Father Meehan adds: "It is amusing to read the highly imaginary descriptions given by many historians of Point du Sable's settlement in Chicago. It has been referred to as a cabin, a small log cabin, a rude cabin, and a rude hut."

This is particularly amusing in view of the inventory accompanying the sale of du Sable's property to Jean Lalime, a French trader, in 1800. It lists a house, 40 feet by 22; a horse mill, 36 by 24; a bakehouse, 20 by 18; and other

Pioneer: Du Sable, the first full-time Chicagoan, remains a figure of some mystery.

structures: a dairy, smokehouse, poultry house, workshop, stable, and barn, the last 40 by 48 feet, with wood enough to build a second barn. Also listed were a crosscut saw with 7-foot blade, a ripsaw, a plane saw, a new plowshare, and a complete plow, as well as a couple of mules, 30 head of cattle, 2 calves, 38 hogs, and almost 4 dozen chickens. Then there were the household furnishings which included a French walnut cabinet with 4 glass doors, 4 tables, a bureau, a large feather bed, a couch, and 7 chairs; a stove, candlesticks, 2 mirrors, 2 paintings, a hatchet, 20 large wooden dishes, 3 basins of pewter and 4 of tin, a coffee mill, scales, 3 copper kettles, a bullet mold, lantern, toasting iron, and 2 copper bells.

Rude hut: For more than six years, du Sable owned the only permanent dwelling on the river.

All in all, quite a hut.

"Undoubtedly," Father Meehan observes, "he owned one of the most complete establishments in the Middle West outside of Detroit and St. Louis."

Historians have called John Kinzie, who bought du Sable's old place from Lalime in 1804, "the first Chicagoan" or "the Father of Chicago." They ignore the impossibility of explaining how anyone buying the house of someone who was there ahead of him can be called "first." Perhaps some have dismissed du Sable cursorily because he was not white and because he lived closely with the local tribes, eventually marrying a Pottawatomie woman. Father Meehan gives short shrift to such attempts, declaring:

> The title and honor of "First Chicagoan" belongs to Jean Baptiste Point du Sable, a man whose claim can be substantiated by at least three contemporary documents. He resided in Chicago for almost 20 years, reared three children there, and even, in the last years of his residence, saw a grandchild born in almost the heart of the present-day city. . . . From this ingenious, resourceful and seemingly well-educated Negro, Chicago draws her permanency.

Du Sable's antecedents are hazy. He may have been a runaway slave from the South or a "base-born descendant" of a black woman and a member of the noted Dandonneau family of France. The more usual guess is that he was a native of Santo Domingo. Andreas supports this hypothesis, writing, "Before settling on the banks of the Chicago River he had lived among the Peorias with a friend named Glamorgan—also a Domingoan—who was reputed to have been possessor of large Spanish land grants near St. Louis, and to the home of this friend he returned to die."

Du Sable sold his place in 1800 and moved to St. Charles, Missouri. During an illness in 1813, he promised to leave his property to his granddaughter, Eulalie, on condition that she care for him in his last years and see that he was buried in the Catholic cemetery at St. Charles.

Whatever the truth of du Sable's ancestry, he was able to prove American citizenship in 1783 in order to obtain a government land grant.

From Nowhere to Nothing

History also records—rather tenuously—that about 1778 a French trader named Guary or Guillory or Guarie arrived in the Chicago area and remained for an unknown time. He is said to have built a house on the west side of the north branch of the Chicago River; according to Gurdon Hubbard (a Chicago newcomer some 40 years later), that portion of the river had once been called ''River Guarie.'' Hubbard said he was shown the reputed site of Guarie's house in 1818. The picket fence—which tradition said surrounded the house—was gone, but the ''corn hills adjoining were distinctly traceable, although overgrown with grass.''

A more tangible figure, Antoine Ouilmette, believed to have been a French-Canadian, came to Chicago in 1796 with his Indian wife. He lived near du Sable until 1829, when his wife was given a plot of land at Gros Point (a few miles north of Chicago) in accordance with a treaty involving her tribe. When the Pottawatomies retreated westward in 1835, Ouilmette and his family moved to Council Bluffs, Iowa, where he died.

Fort Dearborn Is Built: Life was still at hazard in the Northwest Territory as the new century began. In 1803 Gen. Henry Dearborn, secretary of war under President Thomas Jefferson, ordered the building of a number of forts in the Territory. One of these was Chicago, which since 1800 had been part of the newly formed Indiana Territory. Thus, Capt. John Whistler and six men left the fort at Detroit on April 3, 1803 to inspect the Chicago area and choose a site to fortify. He was back in Detroit sometime in mid-July, with plans for the fort in his knapsack.

The captain, who was then 45, had a strange history as a military man. He had been captured by Colonial troops when he was 19 while serving with Burgoyne at Saratoga, and had returned to England after being paroled. But the young Irishman had taken a liking to the infant United States—he quickly returned with his bride. He enlisted in the American army, saw action at the Battle of Fallen Timbers with General Wayne, and was promoted to captain in 1797.

After a short stay in Detroit, Captain Whistler boarded the government schooner *Tracy* en route to his new post. He was accompanied by his wife, Ann, his 19-year-old son, Lt. William Whistler, William's young bride, and another son, George Washington Whistler, age 3. The remainder of the force sent to construct Fort Dearborn, as the new post was named, consisted of Lt. James Strode Swearingen, a young artillery officer, and 67 men. They were to march from Detroit to Chicago, pausing to wait for the *Tracy* at the mouth of the St. Joseph River. The two parties met at the rendezvous point on August 12, although Lt. Swearingen and his troops had to camp for two weeks while the *Tracy* sailed through lakes Erie and Michigan.

As the troops marched around the lake, Captain Whistler and his family completed the 60-mile trip by rowboat. Both parties reached Chicago during the afternoon of August 17. The *Tracy* anchored half a mile offshore, as the entrance to the Chicago River was blocked by a giant sandbar. It had to offload its cargo, including three cannon and other supplies, into small boats to be ferried ashore.

Hundreds of Indians (one estimate says 2,000) found the whole event good theater. They watched the "big canoe with wings" in considerable wonder, and without doubt stared covetously at the huge assortment of articles being stacked—and guarded—on the beach.

Because there were neither horses nor oxen at hand, the men were forced to drag newly cut trees with ropes, no easy task since the fort, though very near the lake, was some eight feet above the river bank. When the fort was finally finished late in 1804, it consisted of two blockhouses (one facing southeast and one northwest), a stone powder magazine, separate quarters for the officers and the men, and a covered sally port leading to the river that could be used for escape and also provided a safe way to ensure the water supply. Outside the walls, which were surrounded by a classic sharpened stockade fence, were houses for the post's Indian agent and the government contractor, as well as the stable and an enclosed space for the fort garden.

A plaque at Michigan Avenue and Wacker Drive now marks the site of Fort Dearborn.

Capt. Thomas G. Anderson, who came to "Millwackie" to trade with the Indians in 1803, recounted his visit to Fort Dearborn while it was still under construction.

> During my second year at Min-na-wack, or Millwackie, Captain Whistler with his company of American soldiers, came to take possession of Chicago. At this time there were no buildings there, except a few dilapidated log huts, covered with bark. Captain Whistler had selected one of these as a temporary, though miserable, residence for his family, his officers and men being under canvas. On being informed of his arrival, I felt it my duty to pay my respects to the authority so much required in this country. On the morrow I mounted Kee-ge-kaw, or Swift-Goer, and the next day I was invited to dine with the captain. On going into the house, the outer door opening into the dining-room, I found the table spread, the family and guests seated, consisting of several ladies, as jolly as kittens.

Early visitors to the fort included various Indian chiefs and traders. Among the latter was a hot-tempered silversmith from Quebec named John

Kinzie; he had arrived from St. Joseph with his wife and infant son and bought the former du Sable place from Lalime. This white "first family" of Chicago was soon expanded by three other children: Ellen Marion, Maria Indiana, and Robert Allen. A. T. Andreas said Kinzie, who started other trading posts at Milwaukee and elsewhere, was "greatly beloved" by the Indians. Their name for him was Shaw-nee-aw-kee, "the Silverman."

Idea man: Tecumseh, famed Indian leader, tried to combine all Indian tribes into a huge anti-settler army. He died fighting for the British.

Trouble Approaches: For about ten years, the Indians had grown increasingly on edge throughout the entire Northwest Territory—in part because the great Tecumseh, chief of the Shawnees, and his erratic brother, the Prophet, had been trying to organize resistance to the white man. But the Pottawatomies and their chiefs—Black Partridge, Winnemeg, Topenebe, and others—usually remained on cordial terms with Kinzie and the Fort Dearborn garrison. In fact, they refused to join an Indian alliance in 1810. The tension would probably have died down in 1811, after the Prophet's resounding defeat at Tippecanoe, but the British took pains to keep it high by wooing the Indians with guns and money. In the middle of this unsteady situation, Captain Whistler was replaced by Capt. Nathaniel Heald, a stubborn New Englander who lacked Whistler's knowledge of Indians.

An uneasy peace lasted until the spring of 1812—then Fort Dearborn went on the alert. A settler named Charles Lee had come to Chicago about the time the fort was built and had started a large farm some four miles from the river's mouth, south of the Forks (the branching of the Chicago River). By 1812, Lee and his family lived near the fort while the farm was managed by Liberty White, with two other men and one of Lee's sons for help. On April 6, 1812, a party of 11 Winnebagoes stopped at the farm and insolently made themselves at home.

One of the farmers whispered that the Indians were not Pottawatomies. A second man, a former soldier, casually told the invaders that he and the youngster were going across the river to feed some cattle and would return shortly. They paddled across the river, made a show of tending the livestock, then slipped into the woods and began running. The Winnebagoes quickly killed the two who had remained behind.

The escaping pair headed for Fort Dearborn, stopping only long enough to warn a family named Burns. When they reached the fort, Ensign George Ronan and others were sent to bring in the Burns family. All the neighboring settlers spent the night within the walls.

The next couple of months saw hit-run raids by roving Indians. Cattle and sheep were stolen. Then, on June 18, 1812, England declared war on the United

Sidekick: Tecumseh's brother, the Prophet, was flakey.

A Short History of Chicago

States. The American fort at Mackinac was unaware of the outbreak of hostilities when the British suddenly attacked on July 16. Mackinac fell without resistance.

Word of the war and the British success at Mackinac reached the Indian tribes at Chicago by runner. Meanwhile, a messenger from Gen. William Hull at Detroit to Captain Heald arrived on August 9 with news of the seizure of Mackinac and orders to evacuate Fort Dearborn as soon as possible. Heald was instructed to distribute surplus supplies to the Indians, presumably to induce them not to hinder the departure.

Heald was in a bad spot. His force consisted of 54 enlisted men and two officers, plus 12 settlers or traders who also were militiamen. Many of the regulars were ill, and Heald had only about 40 men fit for combat. He was further handicapped by the necessity of safeguarding a dozen women and 20 children. The Indians apparently learned of the order to distribute supplies almost as soon as it arrived. Supposedly friendly chiefs began dropping in at mealtime to help eat the surplus food, and on August 12 a group of Indians was shown food, ammunition, and other articles to be given them.

Caught between the devil and the deep blue lake, Heald began considering alternatives—all of them unattractive. Chief Winnemeg of the Pottawatomies, who had brought Hull's message, warned him that his best chance was to stay and fight. Kinzie concurred, but Heald refused. Winnemeg then urged that the fort be abandoned immediately to cut the time during which Indian reinforcements might arrive and an attack be planned. Kinzie added his support. Heald waited.

By this time Pottawatomie chiefs had assured Heald of safe conduct to Fort Wayne in return for the supplies. But Kinzie noticed that despite their friendly words, the visitors always were in "battle array."

On August 13, Captain William Wells and 30 Miami braves rode in from Fort Wayne, a rescue mission for which Wells had volunteered when he heard of Heald's plight. And on August 14, the day before the scheduled evacuation, Black Partridge showed up at Heald's headquarters to return the medal he had been given at Greenville by General Wayne 20 years earlier. Black Partridge explained, or so the story runs: "Father, I come to deliver up to you the medal I won. It was given me by the Americans and I have long worn it in token of our mutual friendship. But our young men are resolved to imbue their hands in the blood of the whites. I cannot restrain them, and I will not wear a token of peace while I am compelled to act as an enemy."

After listening to his advisers, among them Kinzie and Wells, Heald decided to destroy the liquor and any excess rifles and ammunition, leaving everything else for the Indians. The destruction was begun. That same evening

William Wells, a native of Kentucky, had been kidnapped as a boy and adopted by Chief Little Turtle of the Miamis. With the arrival of General Wayne in Indiana, he realized that he might soon be fighting against his own Kentucky kinsmen. Wells reportedly addressed Little Turtle with great emotion: "We will be friends until the sun reaches the midday height. From that time we will be enemies; and if you want to kill me then, you may. And if I want to kill you, I may."

An Indian gentleman: Black Partridge, given a medal by "Mad Anthony" Wayne 20 years earlier, returned it to the army in 1812 because he could do nothing to stop the Fort Dearborn attack.

Kinzie left the fort to wash himself at the river. He was seized in the twilight by two Indians lurking outside, who quickly recognized and released him. But they also asked why they heard hammering and noise inside the walls. Kinzie calmly explained that the troops were opening barrels of pork and flour to get supplies for the march, and the Indians seemed satisfied. As a result, however, the liquor, powder, and smashed rifles were thrown into the well inside the covered sally port, hidden from Indian eyes.

Massacre: The scene when the gates of Fort Dearborn swung open at 9 o'clock on the morning of August 15 was in the finest tradition of scriptwriters yet unborn. Captain Wells, in Indian garb, his face blackened in the manner of an Indian going into battle, was leading the cortege with 15 of the Miamis. The garrison was next, followed by two slow-moving ox-drawn wagons holding most of the women and children, although several other women were on horseback. The rear was guarded by the militiamen and 15 other Miami warriors.

For some eerie reason, the two fifers and two drummers who comprised the garrison band struck up the "Dead March" as they emerged from the fort.

Kinzie, who had sent his family by boat to the river mouth with instructions to leave only when told to do so, was with the soldiers in hopes that his long friendship with the Indians might have a calming effect. (This was in spite of ominous warnings by several Pottawatomie chieftains not to take part in the withdrawal.) Looting of the fort began as soon as the last person was through the gate.

The departure route, an old Indian trail, paralleled the lake for a while. About a mile and a half from the fort, Wells and others noticed Indian maneuvers that seemed to indicate an ambush a short distance ahead and to the west, behind a ridge of sandhills. Wells raced to tell Captain Heald, who immediately ordered a charge up the sandy slope. The Indians opened fire when the first soldiers appeared over the top. An estimated 500 Indians soon closed all escape routes, and the massacre was on with no doubt at all about the issue.

When the first rifle shots sounded, the Miamis rode off. Kinzie, reliving the scene at the battle site eight years later, remembered a Miami brave who was half-Pottawatomie pausing long enough to berate the attackers: "Pottawatomie, I am much astonished at your conduct. You have been treacherous with these people. You have deceived them and are about to murder them in cold blood. Let me advise you to beware. You know not what evil the dead shall bring upon you, you may bye and bye hear your wives and children cry and you will not be able to assist them. Pottawatomie beware."

How Kinzie could have heard this angry speech is never made clear, but if the Miami had time for such words, it would seem ample proof that the 30 Indians who accompanied Wells from Fort Wayne were not fleeing in panic. Instead, they simply were riding away from what, as professionals, they knew was a hopeless situation.

Brief journey: The party evacuating Fort Dearborn got as far as the sand hills (just above the letter L) before the Indians ambushed.

CHICAGO IN 1812.

From Nowhere to Nothing

21

The one-sided conflict lasted no more than 15 minutes. Wells fought with such savage bravery that he probably killed eight of the 15 Indian dead before, trapped under his fallen horse, he was knifed or shot in the back and killed. By most accounts of this kaleidoscopic slaughter, the Indians then paid him the ultimate tribute. They cut out his heart and ate it in hopes of acquiring his courage.

No one can truly know what happened during the confusion. In a well-known account, Kinzie's stepdaughter, Mrs. Margaret Helm, recalls grappling with a young warrior who was trying to tomahawk her. She then recounts that an older Indian shoved her assailant aside and dragged her, still struggling, into the lake—where he stopped with her head just above water. She said she stood quietly after she recognized that her savior was Black Partridge, the Kinzie family friend. Kinzie, however, remembers Mrs. Helm remaining with him during the battle until Black Partridge appeared, when she ran in panic into the lake and remained until she was reassured. The chief then took Kinzie's rifle and escorted him and his stepdaughter to a place of safety beyond the fort.

Captain Heald's wife, Rebekah, wounded several times, was aboard her beautiful bay mare from Kentucky, the one every Indian coveted, until the reins were seized and she was led away. Then a squaw ran up and tried to take a blanket she was holding. Rebekah began slashing at the woman with a whip, while the Indian warriors watched her defiant response approvingly.

Within minutes of the initial attack, Ensign Ronan and Captain Wells were dead, as were the post surgeon and the soldier who fatally bayoneted an Indian chief, Naunongee, during hand-to-hand combat. Meanwhile, a fierce and merciless rifle, knife, and tomahawk raid on the wagons brought death to the 12 militiamen, 2 women, and 12 of the children. By this time Heald recognized that the situation was hopeless. With his battered force—now dwindled to perhaps 25 enlisted men and noncoms—he broke through to a slight elevation out of range of the Indian guns.

The Captives' Fate: Black Bird, chief of the attacking mob, sent an emissary to Heald asking for surrender. The captain requested a conference, which was granted. It began, oddly enough, with a handshake. Heald demanded assurances of safety for all who surrendered and agreed to pay the $100 requested. The surrender terms supposedly protected all but the gravely wounded.

The fighting had ended, but not the dying. As the prisoners huddled together awaiting their various fates, some of the victorious Indians raised rifles in preparation for a volley in honor of their own dead. This caused an alarmed (and obviously unsearched) captive to draw a concealed knife. The Indians thereupon fired into the group, killing three. During that afternoon and evening, some of those most seriously wounded were slain—often after torture—while those unhurt or only slightly wounded were apportioned to various tribal chiefs, presumably to be ransomed later.

Through the influence of Black Partridge and other chiefs, Kinzie and his family were given special treatment. They were permitted to return home while the Indians debated their fate and that of Captain Heald and his wife. Despite Black Bird's promise, many wanted to kill Heald. Not only was he the most important prisoner, but—more to the point—he had destroyed the guns and liquor the Indians had been led to expect. Furthermore, during one of the councils, with both Kinzie and Heald present, a brave accused them of poisoning the flour left for the Indians.

Kinzie pointed out that Heald's superior officer had sent orders about the supplies which Heald had to obey. He quietly added that if they would bring him some of the supposedly poisonous flour, he would eat it himself. The Pottawatomie leaders, perhaps uneasy at the memory of the warning from the departing Miami, admitted treachery and asked whether the President would forgive them for the attack.

That same afternoon, an Indian friend warned Kinzie to get Heald out of the way quickly or he would be killed. Kinzie told his half-Indian clerk to take the Healds by canoe to St. Joseph at once. Although this was done secretly, angry warriors soon discovered the escape and pursued the swift war canoe for 15 miles across the lake before giving up the chase.

The next day, August 16, the Indians burned Fort Dearborn. Three hundred miles away, General Hull (later to be cashiered for cowardice) surrendered the fort at Detroit to the British without firing a shot.

A couple of days after the massacre, a group of Indians with black-painted faces—who had arrived too late to take part—came to the Kinzie home on some obscure pretext. Fortunately, some of the Pottawatomie chiefs were present. They persuaded the strangers to depart after giving them food and gifts. This story also has a variant, later recounted by Kinzie's daughter-in-law, Juliette.

At this moment a friendly war-whoop was heard from a party of newcomers on the opposite bank of the river. Black Partridge sprang to meet their leader. "Who are you?" . . . "I am the Sauganash" [the "Englishman"]. "Then make haste to the house. Your friend is in danger; you alone can save him." Billy Caldwell—for it was he—entered with a calm step and

Mrs. Juliette Kinzie: Imaginative author of "Waubun."

without a trace of agitation. He deliberately took off his accoutrements and placed them with his rifle behind the door, then saluted the hostile savages:

"How now, my friends! A good day to you! I was told there were enemies here; but I am glad to find only friends. Why have you blackened your faces? Is it that you are in mourning for the friends you lost in battle? Or is it that you are fasting? If so, ask our friend here and he will give you to eat. He is the Indians' friend, and never yet refused them what they had need of."

Thus taken by surprise, the savages were ashamed to acknowledge their bloody purpose. They, therefore, said modestly they had come to beg of their friends some white cotton cloth in which to wrap their dead.

Accuracy was not Juliette Kinzie's strong point—as many who have checked her stories will attest. But she did know how to dress up a lackluster anecdote.

Aftermath: On the third day after the massacre, the Kinzies were permitted to leave by boat for St. Joseph. There they were for a time under the protection of Chief Topenebe, a brother-in-law of one of the Chicago traders. Mrs. Kinzie and Margaret Helm continued on to Detroit in November and reported to British General Procter, who granted them parole and let them live in the city. After some weeks trading in St. Joseph in an effort to recoup his losses at Fort Dearborn, Kinzie came to Detroit in December or January and also received parole.

In the meantime Captain and Mrs. Heald had been taken to Mackinac by Alexander Robinson (Chechepinqua), a Pottawatomie chief. From there they finally managed to reach Detroit and, eventually, their home in Louisville. There are a couple of footnotes to their story: Twelve days after the massacre, Heald learned that he had been promoted to major. And when he and his wife reached Louisville, they received a package containing jewelry that had been taken from them. There was a large silver blanket pin, initialed RAM, Rebekah's breastpin, and her tortoiseshell comb mounted in gold. The items, sold or traded by the Indians, were purchased by a friend in a store in St. Louis.

It was a couple of months before Lt. Helm, another member of the Fort Dearborn contingent, was known to be safe in an Indian village on the Kankakee River. Black Partridge was authorized to go there and offer "two mules and a barrle (sic) of stuff [whisky]" for Helm's freedom. The chief went, but was told the price was too low. He promptly threw in his own horse and rifle

Chechepinqua: On joining
the Chicago Temperance
Society in January 1834, he
is said to have pulled a
bottle of whiskey from his
pocket and smashed it with
a tomahawk.

and, for a last tipping of the scales, the golden ornament he wore in his nose.

On October 5, 1813, almost a year before the decisive American naval victory on Lake Champlain, Tecumseh—now a British brigadier general—led his Indians beside General Procter's troops at the Battle of the Thames. Outnumbered and without naval help, Procter was defeated by General Harrison. Tecumseh, one of the greatest of the Indian leaders, was slain. With the loss of Tecumseh and the end of the War of 1812, midwestern Indians lacked the heart to continue their long battle against the encroaching whites. There were sporadic uprisings, but little real hope.

To return briefly to Fort Dearborn: "For four years the charred and blackened ruins of the fort remained, and the bodies of the slain lay unburied where they fell." Chicago seemingly had no future of any consequence.

Back to Square One

3

Time moved slowly and unremarkably during the next three or four years in what remained of Chicago after the killing ended and the Indians had vanished to their various villages. Fort Dearborn was a jumbled rubbish heap, with only the brick powder magazine standing perpetual guard. No bugles keened or commanded. No cannon gave boisterous welcome to the morning sun, or roared farewell when evening came. "Aside from visits of traders with Mackinac goods," wrote historian Bessie Louise Pierce, "and the occasional passage of war parties to assail the American frontier, Chicago lapsed into a prairie wilderness, no longer a place of human habitation."

Yet Chicago was not completely deserted.

Antoine Ouilmette and his family still occupied their cabin west of the Kinzie place, although Ouilmette, in the words of Andreas, "was left the only white inhabitant of Chicago." Ouilmette—who obviously didn't think in terms of color—lived with his Indian wife and a number of children, and by 1814 his friend, Alexander Robinson (Chief Chechepinqua), was back. A year later he and Ouilmette were planting corn together in the abandoned Fort Dearborn garden. In the same year, John Dean, an army contractor, built a home on the lakefront near the mouth of the river.

Other settlers and traders began drifting in, realizing that Fort Dearborn would be replaced. Some were survivors with bitter memories; others were newcomers. Jean Baptiste Beaubien, who would become a leading citizen, was one of the latter. Late in 1812 he bought the Lee cabin near the ruined fort, and married the young daughter of a nearby trader.

Beaubien, born in Detroit in 1780, had been a successful fur buyer for years. He had two sons by his first wife, Mah-naw-buh-no-quah, an Ottawa Indian who had died in Milwaukee. Beaubien owned trading posts there and

Opposite page
Spreading out: Fort Dearborn (center) and Kinzie's place (right foreground) with Wolf Point upriver a piece.

in Green Bay before adding the place in Chicago. He spent much of his time traveling.

The Flag Flies Once More: The tiny settlement was greatly cheered when two companies of infantry under command of Capt. Hezekiah Bradley arrived on July 4, 1816, to begin construction of a new Fort Dearborn. Bradley brought a group of skilled workmen as well as an army engineer, Lt. William S. Evileth, to serve as architect and oversee the work. Captain Bradley quickly arranged the burial of those killed four years before. He also bought the 1816 corn crop from Ouilmette and Robinson for the garrison. Work on the fort was completed in May 1817 when Brevet Major Daniel Baker became the commandant.

Evileth left for other duties in November and was drowned when his ship went down off Indiana, near the Calumet River. Everyone aboard perished.

Others who arrived in 1816 included the Kinzie family, Lt. Helm and his wife, Margaret, Charles Jouett, a six-foot three-inch former Indian agent, back after a dozen years or so, and Jacob B. Varnum, in charge of the government store.

With the fort operational again, Conant and Mack, a Detroit firm, sent John Crafts to Chicago with a supply of trading goods—including plenty of liquor. He established a post in the cabin at the unoccupied Lee farm. This was south of the Forks on the west bank of the river along the usual route of Indian traders in the area. It was the scene of the killings that preluded the massacre.

Mrs. Lee had been captured with her infant child during the attack and taken to Black Partridge's village, where she was well treated. She and her child were ransomed some weeks later by M. DuPin, a French trader. They later married and lived in the Kinzie cabin.

Kinzie resumed his profession of silversmith and tried to reestablish his profitable fur trade. But competition from the American Fur Company, established in 1809 by John Jacob Astor of New York, was formidable. Neither government stores (commonly called "factories") nor private traders unaffiliated with what Astor soon turned into a virtual monopoly stood much chance of success. Fortunately for his purse, Kinzie also had been named subagent and interpreter for the Indian Agency.

One improvement at the new fort was the establishment of a school. The first Fort Dearborn, in the winter of 1810–11, had had a class in spelling for a lone pupil, 6-year-old John H. Kinzie. The teacher was Robert A. Forsyth, 13, and spelling was the only subject taught because a spelling book had somehow reached the fort in the middle of a chest of tea. The second Fort Dearborn had William L. Cox, a retired soldier, as teacher. His classes in the fall of 1817 consisted of young Kinzie, now 12, his two smaller sisters and a brother, and three or four youngsters from military families. There is no record of the curriculum or how long the school continued.

In 1816 Jean Baptiste Beaubien purchased contractor Dean's house. He paid $1,000 for this "low, gloomy building of five rooms," and his son,

A Short History of Chicago

Alexander, was born there. Beaubien went to work for the American Fur Company and became a permanent resident of Chicago in 1819. Chicago's first recorded baptism took place three years later; the Rev. Stephen A. Badin, visiting for the second time, christened Alexander at Fort Dearborn.

Illinois was admitted to the Union in 1818 as the twenty-first state when it had about 40,000 residents. The state capital was first Kaskaskia and then Vandalia, an indication of reluctance to bet on the future of Chicago, regarded, according to Finis Farr, only as a "village of fur traders dependent on a military post." And around the fort, relations between the Indians and whites gradually fell into the old pattern, as Andreas suggests, with the Pottawatomie chiefs again welcomed "around the homes and firesides of their friends." Among them was Black Partridge, whose village had been destroyed by a punitive expedition and his people slaughtered or chased away. As before, the settlers planted, hunted, and bartered with trading vessels for supplies. "Thus the days on the frontier passed away."

Indian Sunset: Life in Chicago was quiet, but efforts to force the Indians further west picked up speed. In 1816 the Treaty of St. Louis provided for the surrender of an area surrounding the lower end of Lake Michigan, ten miles north and ten miles south of "the Chicago creek," as well as other lands back to the Kankakee, Illinois, and Fox rivers.

Eighteen twenty-one saw another stage in the seemingly endless acquisitions of land by the whites. Three or four thousand Indians gathered in Chicago while chieftains of the Pottawatomies-of-the-Woods, Ottawas, and Chippewas (probably once a single tribe) met with a government commission headed by Gov. Lewis Cass of Michigan—who came to Chicago by canoe. The council was held on the north bank of the river, near the homes of Kinzie and Dr. Alexander Wolcott. The pow-wow lasted about a week, and the treaty was signed only after further delay by the reluctant Pottawatomies. The tribes ceded five million acres in southwestern Michigan to the United States and also yielded land for the building of roads from Detroit and Fort Wayne to Chicago.

In return, the Pottawatomies were promised $5,000 annually for 20 years and the services at Chicago of a blacksmith and schoolteacher. The other tribes were given smaller amounts. The fact that game was growing scarcer and the fur trade declining undoubtedly played a part in the Indians' decision.

By 1822 the American Fur Company had captured most of the trade, and the government factories closed down—partially as a result of Astor's lobbying in Congress. The New York concern bought the Fort Dearborn trading post for $500 and resold it to Beaubien, who was back in business for himself. In 1828 all

Father Badin, who entered the priesthood in Baltimore in 1793, is said to have been the first Catholic priest ordained in the United States.

Dr. Wolcott became the son-in-law of John Kinzie. He and Ellen Marion Kinzie, usually accorded the title of the "first white child" born in Chicago, were married July 20, 1823. It was the first Chicago wedding.

other American Fur Company property in Chicago was sold to 26-year-old Gurdon S. Hubbard, who had come to Chicago from Montreal in 1818 as an apprentice to the company for five years at an annual wage of $120. Hubbard, a Vermont native, was the perfect model for the All-American Boy and fitted into the frontier scene superbly. He liked the Indians, and they admired him. They called him Pa-ea-ma-ta-be ("the Swift Walker"), and he is said to have covered 75 miles on foot in a single day.

The Swift Walker: Gurdon Hubbard, fur-trader, packer, prominent Chicagoan, once walked 75 miles in a day.

Anvil Chorus: The 1821 agreement with the Indians providing a blacksmith in Chicago was implemented in June 1823. David McKee, a 23-year-old native of Virginia, was brought from Cincinnati by Benjamin Kerchival, the Indian agent. McKee built a house on the north side of the river and, in 1827, added the duties of mail courier to his blacksmithing. The new mailman made monthly trips between Fort Dearborn and Fort Wayne by way of Niles, Michigan and Elkhart, Indiana. His horse carried the mailbags and camping equipment while the tireless McKee walked, using his rifle to provide food. The average round trip took 14 days—although he once did the distance in 10.

Among visitors to Chicago in 1823 was Prof. William H. Keating, a mineralogist from the University of Pennsylvania who forgot to bring along his rose-colored glasses. Keating viewed the town with a supercilious eye and promptly established himself as world class in the unsound-judgment category by writing:

The climate of Chicago seems to have changed radically during its 150 years' existence. In 1823 Keating observed, "The maize seldom has time to ripen, owing to the shortness and coldness of the season."

> The village presents no cheering prospect, as, not withstanding its antiquity, it consists of but few huts, inhabited by a miserable race of men, scarcely equal to the Indians from whom they are descended. Their log or bark houses are low, filthy and disgusting, displaying not the least trace of comfort . . .
>
> As a place of business, it offers no inducement to the settler; for the whole annual shipment of the trade on the lake did not exceed the cargo of five or six schooners, even at the time when the garrison received its supplies from Mackinaw . . . the dangers attending the navigation of the lake, and the scarcity of harbors along the shore, must ever prove a serious obstacle to the increase of the commercial importance of Chicago.

Fort Dearborn was evacuated again in 1823, this time peaceably. Dr. Wolcott was left in charge, and the fort itself was occupied mostly by *voyageurs* and their families, or emigrants pausing in Chicago before continuing west. Meanwhile, a few new Chicago residents were arriving from the East.

A Short History of Chicago

War Drums Again: In the fall of 1828 there were rumors of impending trouble with the Indians. But the tribes came in, as always, for their September annuities. After payment in the usual silver half-dollars, the visitors—except Big Foot and his Wisconsin Pottawatomies—went home. The night after their departure, while the settlers held a dance in the enlisted men's barracks, lightning set fire to the building.

The flames were seen by Mrs. Helm, sleeping at the Kinzie house just across the river. She awakened Hubbard and Robert Kinzie, who hurried to the river only to find their canoe partially submerged. Both swam the river and ran to the fort, where two barracks buildings and a storehouse were ablaze. The guardhouse at the east was also starting to smolder; Kinzie, wrapping himself in a water-soaked blanket, climbed to the roof. About 40 men and women formed a bucket brigade from the river's edge, and Kinzie fought the flames until daylight despite his badly burned hands and face.

Significantly, none of Big Foot's tribesmen offered to help, although they stood and watched. They departed the next morning for Lake Geneva.

A few days later the Kinzie household heard the sound of distant singing on the river. Soon a large canoe came into view. Its passengers included Gov. Lewis Cass and his secretary, Robert Forsyth. They had come from the Chicago Portage to tell of the massacre of white settlers along the Mississippi by roving Winnebagoes, whom Big Foot was known to favor joining.

Hubbard asked the two friendly Pottawatomie chiefs, Shawbonee and Billy Caldwell (the "Sauganash") to learn Big Foot's intentions. The two went to Lake Geneva, where Caldwell hid while Shawbonee walked into camp alone to a hostile reception. Big Foot accused him of spying for the white man and Shawbonee angrily responded that even if the Winnebagoes and Big Foot joined forces, their cause would be hopeless. He promised, however, to listen to their thoughts, then return to his people and do whatever they wished.

Big Foot agreed, but sent one of his braves to Chicago with Shawbonee. The latter, not wishing it known that Caldwell was nearby, began complaining about his treatment by Big Foot as they neared Caldwell's hiding place. He added in a loud voice, "We must have no one with us in going to Chicago. Should we meet any of your band, *or anyone else*, we must tell them to go away; we must go by ourselves and get to Chicago by noon tomorrow."

Caldwell got the message and returned to Chicago by a different trail. At the Pottawatomie council, he and Shawbonee persuaded their tribesmen not to support Big Foot or the Winnebagoes.

There still was unease among the Chicago settlers, and Hubbard went to the Danville area to seek help. He was back in seven days with 100 men from along the Vermilion River. During that time he had traveled approximately 250 miles on horseback and swum several rivers. In his absence Jean Baptiste Beaubien organized a 50-man militia force.

Thirty days later word reached Chicago that General Cass had routed the Winnebagoes and signed a peace treaty. But in October 1828 Fort Dearborn was garrisoned once more. It remained occupied, except for a brief period in 1832, until it was abandoned permanently on May 10, 1837.

Frenchman with a fiddle: Mark Beaubien was a hotel owner, race horse enthusiast, violinist . . . and perhaps the most genial man in town.

In 1825-26 Chicago had 14 registered taxpayers and 35 voters, of whom 21 were French. The town had $8,000 worth of taxable property with $6,000 owned by the American Fur Company. At the time real estate was not taxed.

The Frenchman Cometh: One of everyone's favorite characters reached Chicago in 1826. The 26-year-old Mark Beaubien hired an Indian guide and drove his team along the trail from Detroit to Chicago to visit his brother, Jean Baptiste. Then he decided to bring his family and stay. "There was no town laid out," Mark later remembered. "Didn't expect no town. When they laid out the town, my house was laid out in the middle of the street."

John H. Fonda of Prairie du Chien, Wisconsin, who visited Chicago briefly the year before Beaubien arrived, gave a similar picture of the tiny settlement: "At that time, Chicago was merely an Indian agency. It contained about fourteen houses, and not more than seventy-five or one hundred inhabitants at the most. . . . The staple business seemed to be carried on by the Indians and runaway soldiers, who hunted ducks and muskrats in the marshes. The principal inhabitants were the agent [Dr. Wolcott], a Mr. Hubbard, a Frenchman by the name of Ouilmette, and John B. Beaubien."

Mark Beaubien bought a log house from James Kinzie at the southeast corner of Lake and Market streets, near the Forks, and opened a hotel. He soon built a large frame addition to serve both as hotel and dwelling. It was "a pretentious white two-story building with bright blue shutters."

Billy Caldwell happened past as Mark worked on the addition and said, "I suppose you will name your hotel after some great man, as the Americans do." "Yes," Beaubien told him. "I will name it after a great man. I shall call it the 'Sauganash.'"

Beaubien ran the tavern until 1834, and it was one of Chicago's most popular hostelries for many years. It burned down in 1851.

Beaubien's love for enjoyment, preferably shared with others, his unfailing good humor, and an extraordinary devotion to the violin made him welcome everywhere. (He may also hold the Chicago record for the most progeny: 23 children, 53 grandchildren, and an uncounted number of great-grandchildren.) Andreas wrote of him:

Mr. Beaubien is described as being in his prime, "a tall, athletic, fine-appearing man, Frenchy and polite, frank, open-hearted, generous to a

A Short History of Chicago

Beaubien's pride: Built in 1831 by Mark Beaubien, the Sauganash Hotel was Chicago's first frame building.

fault, and, in his glory at a horse-race.'' His favorite dress on ''great occasions'' was a swallow-tail coat with brass buttons, and, if in the summer, light nankeen trousers. His quaint old song, in regard to the surrender of Gen. Hull at Detroit in 1812, of which he was a witness, was sung with as much gusto as Monie Musk and Fisher's Hornpipe were played.

The cheerful Beaubien once declared that he ''kept tavern like hell,'' and who could ask for a better memorial: ''He brought a violin with him, and with it he made more hearts merry than any man who ever lived in Chicago.''

Progress on Several Fronts: Even before Illinois became a state in 1818, there had been talk about an Illinois and Michigan Canal to provide direct passage between Lake Michigan and New Orleans via the Chicago River and the Mississippi. In 1829 the project seemed close to a beginning. The Illinois legislature provided for appointment of a three-man Canal Commission whose duties included establishing town sites along the right-of-way between Chicago and La Salle. The federal government had two years earlier granted vast areas of land adjoining the proposed route; the commission was empowered to sell lots to help finance the canal.

Ottawa, at the junction of the Fox and Illinois rivers, was the first town laid out. Chicago, at the other end, was plotted in 1830 by James Thompson, a canal surveyor. The few lots sold in Chicago in 1831 to defray the costs of the survey included two on which Mark Beaubien built the Sauganash—they cost him a

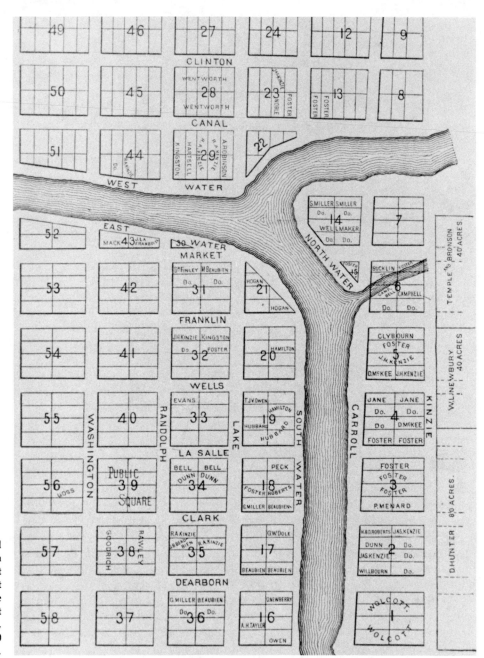

Planning: Prior to its formal survey, Chicago had been a kind of Topsy-town that "growed" by itself. Now it had streets, and the ownership of this or that property was shown. Still, there were fewer than 100 inhabitants.

A Short History of Chicago

total of $100. Jean Baptiste Beaubien also bought two for $102, and Gurdon Hubbard paid only $75 for two more.

In the next few years, a number of schools were established, most of them private (or nearly so). One, in the old Dean-Beaubien house, accommodated pupils from the ages of 4 to 20 and drew from both town and garrison. In 1832 a small school was subsidized by popular subscription in the Indian Agency house, midway between the lake and Wolf Point, as the Forks were known. Many contributing were childless, and enough was pledged to pay for 30 pupils, although only a dozen enrolled the first quarter—of whom eight were part Indian. Billy Caldwell offered to pay all tuition and buy books for Indian children attending, but only if they would wear American clothes, which he also would pay for. There were no takers.

Schoolmarm: Early teacher Eliza Chappel taught 20 pupils in a house near the fort in 1833.

The schoolhouse was a former stable, 12 feet square; its furniture consisted of benches and desks made from old store boxes. John Watkins, a newcomer to town, was the teacher. But the growing town was beginning to need a building designed solely as a school. Three years later, such a building went up on Clark Street near Lake. It was paid for by John S. Wright (who later became the public-spirited publisher of the *Prairie Farmer*). Tuition was $2 a quarter, waived if the parents could not pay.

The ideal school disciplinarian may have been one Edward Murphy. In 1837 he took over the classes and the North Side lease of John Brown, who had been seriously beaten by some of his students. Murphy immediately told the 36 students that he expected obedience.

> The day after, I placed an oak sapling, an inch in diameter, on my desk. That afternoon a Mr. S., who owned the building, came into the school-room, and seeing the walls decorated with caricatures, and likenesses of almost every animal from a rabbit to an elephant, he got in a raging passion, and used rather abusive language. I complained, he became more violent. I walked to my desk, took the sapling and shouted "clear out," which he obeyed by a rapid movement. This trifling incident effectually calmed the ringleaders, some of whom now occupy honorable and respectable positions in society.

Between 1800 and 1818 Chicago was part of either the Indiana or Illinois territories. After Illinois became a state in 1818, Chicago was, successively, in the counties of Crawford, Clark, Pike, Fulton, Putnam (attached to Peoria), and finally Cook—which included what are now Lake, McHenry, DuPage, and Will counties.

Chicago's population was about 200 by the end of 1831, the year Cook County was created. That April a special term of the Court of Cook County Commissioners established the tax rate of one-half of 1 percent "on town lots, on pleasure carriages, on distilleries, on all horses, mules and neat cattle above the age of three years; on watches, with all their appurtenances; and on all clocks." The commissioners also licensed certain merchants and tavern keepers and established prices: half-pints of wine, rum or brandy, 25 cents; break-

Nostalgia, early Chicago style: Kinzie's mansion in 1832.

fast or supper, 25 cents; dinner, 37½ cents; feed for horse, 25 cents; night's lodging, 50 cents (horse) or 12½ cents (man); cider and beer, 6¼ cents per pint.

James Kinzie was licensed as an auctioneer; he soon made $14.54 commission selling $1,153.75 worth of Chicago land. Mark Beaubien was approved to run a ferry near the Forks after posting a surety bond and paying a fee. Cook County residents were to ride free "with their traveling apratus [sic]." Other rates remained what they were for an earlier ferry that had been operated nearby: foot passengers, 6¼ cents; man and horse, 12½ cents; one-horse wagon, 25 cents; four-wheeled carriage, drawn by two oxen or horses, 37½ cents; head of neat cattle or mules, 10 cents; hog, sheep, or goat, 3 cents. Beaubien, who sometimes failed to run the ferry when there was a horse race handy, soon was rebuked by the commissioners. They ordered that the ferry be in operation "from daylight in the morning until dark, without stopping."

Less than a year later, the militia helped build a bridge across the south branch of the Chicago River. Citizens contributed $286.20 toward the cost, and the Pottawatomies gave another $200. Although of solid construction and immovable, the bridge quickly fell into disrepair; the more free-wheeling passersby began treating it as a source of firewood. It was officially demolished

A Short History of Chicago

in 1840. A footbridge also was built over the north branch in 1832, and a drawbridge was thrown across the river at Dearborn Street in the summer of 1834 to permit Chicagoans to pass from one section of their town to another.

Chicago's first public building went up in 1832. It was an estray pen for loose livestock. The contract was awarded after a bid of $20, of which only $12 was paid because of an argument with the builder. The first jail, made of logs, was built in 1833, the year a meeting of citizens voted 12 to 1 to incorporate as a town.

The lone dissenter was Russel E. Heacock, an eccentric citizen who came to Chicago in 1827. After living for some time in the unoccupied fort, he bought a cabin at Hardscrabble, outside of the proposed town limits. At various times Heacock was a carpenter, Chicago's first lawyer, a member of the road commission, a tavern keeper and a justice of the peace. He also was an early subscriber to the *Chicago Democrat*—the town's first newspaper—launched November 26, 1833, by John Calhoun as a Whig weekly.

The paper's motto was: "Where Liberty dwells, there is my Country"—a pronouncement credited to Benjamin Franklin.

The May 9, 1834, issue of the *Chicago Democrat* carried a notice from the town authorities that henceforth there would be a fine of $5 for anyone riding or driving across a bridge any faster than a walk. Since the town had no constables, half of the fine was to be given to the informant.

Despite the increased rate of Chicago's growth—350 residents in 1833, an estimated 1,800 a year later—the spurt in building, the appearance (at least) of urbanization, and dozens of other signs that both fur-trading and Fort Dearborn were about to become anomalies, there was to be a final confrontation with an angry Indian chief. It was brought about by a misunderstanding on the Indian side and accidental or perhaps deliberate misrepresentation on the part of the whites. Liquor also played a part, but on this occasion it was the paleface who overindulged.

Black Hawk Doesn't Live Here Any More: This last Indian threat to Chicago and the surrounding countryside came in 1832 from Black Hawk, one of the chiefs of the combined Sacs and Foxes. The chief complained that white settlers had occupied his village and the surrounding farmland in 1831 while his band was off hunting. The whites, arguing that the Indians had ceded the land by treaty, even appropriated crops the tribe had planted. But the Indians were determined to return to their home. Black Hawk, in fact, had never signed the treaty with his tribe.

Reading the treaty with different eyes, Gov. John Reynolds declared that Illinois had been invaded and requested federal help. Black Hawk was soon defeated and his village burned. Driven back across the Mississippi, he was

Proud but ill-starred: Black Hawk lost his land, people, and hope.

forced to sign a new treaty. Black Hawk now agreed to remain west of the big river, and to relinquish forever any claim to his ancestral lands.

He might have stuck to the bargain, except that fortune was against him. The following year—1832—was a bad one. Having lost their last season's crop completely, Black Hawk and his band were short of food, ammunition, and supplies, and they did not have money to pay trading accounts. As a result, when Black Hawk was invited by the Winnebagoes to plant some of their land in Illinois, he accepted.

Again he led his people into their lost area, but this time it was obvious he wasn't planning for war. Everyone and everything came: "Old men, women, and children, warriors, ponies and household goods, as was common to the tribe when making a peaceful migration." Fewer than 400 of the total party of about 1,600 were fighting men.

Once over the river, Black Hawk broke the group into smaller units and sent them to a number of friendly Indian villages. He himself headed for the Winnebago country with more noncombatants than braves. But nervous settlers sent a hurry-up call to Fort Armstrong at Rock Island, and they organized a force of 1,800 militiamen as defenders until the regulars could arrive. An editorial in the Galena, Illinois, *Galenian* suggested that since Black Hawk had split his band among the neighboring tribes, the militia ought to disband in response to his evident desire to avoid a confrontation. Nevertheless, on May 10, about 400 militiamen under the command of Isaiah Stillman were following the trail of "the half-starved remnant of the migratory tribe," intending to eliminate the Indians once and for all.

Two days later, learning that Stillman and his men were nearby, Black Hawk sent a small party of mounted braves under a flag of truce to the militia encampment at White Rock Grove (about 35 miles from the present town of Dixon). In Andreas's words, Black Hawk did not know that the soldiers "had with them a full commissary supply, including a barrel of whisky, and authorities are unanimous in saying that many of them were inspired by the maudlin courage they had imbibed."

As soon as Stillman's small outpost saw Indians approaching, the soldiers ran for their horses and rode out shooting. Two Indians were killed; two were captured and later slain. The survivors turned and raced back to their own camp, hotly pursued by the militiamen. Here the scenario suddenly changed. Enraged by the death of their fellows, Black Hawk's braves came swarming from camp to chase the enemy back to its base. A battle began, but the militia, though superior in number, fled in disorder, leaving 11 dead and giving their campsite a new and derisive name: "Stillman's Run."

Black Hawk and his band now were definitely on the warpath. The Indian

A Short History of Chicago

leader fashioned small raiding parties which began hitting white settlements. Stillman's routed militia were ordered disbanded, and virtually every white settler west and north of Chicago began heading there for protection.

The Army Arrives: Maj. William Whistler, who had helped his father build the first Fort Dearborn 28 years earlier, was ordered from Fort Niagara to garrison Chicago. Gen. Winfield Scott and troops were loaded on ships in Buffalo and sent to join the fight against Black Hawk. And a detachment of militia came riding in from Michigan to serve as a Chicago defense force until the army arrived.

Early in June, the never-say-die Big Foot again was campaigning for a general Indian uprising against the whites. He spoke in words of fire to a council of Indian leaders, which also was attended by Col. Thomas J. V. Owen, the Indian agent in charge of Fort Dearborn. Colonel Owen responded moderately, pointing out what the Indians would lose in the way of annuities, land, and other benefits, since they would surely be defeated. Big Foot, boasting of the size of the force which all the Indians together could muster, said it would rival the number of trees in the forest. Shawbonee replied, "Your army would equal in number the trees in the forest, and you would encounter an army of palefaces as numerous as the leaves on those trees." End of argument.

Hastily organized Chicago militiamen searched the countryside for settlers needing assistance, or for Indian war parties. None saw action, although one expedition had the grisly task of burying 15 men, women, and children tortured and slain at Indian Creek near Ottawa. During much of June Chicago was host to about 500 refugees, most of them living in Fort Dearborn or shanties nearby.

Major Whistler and some troops arrived on June 16 from Fort Niagara, ousting most of the refugees from the fort, which had to be made ready for the arrival of General Scott and his men. Asiatic cholera had broken out on two of the four ships in the Scott expedition, however, and these vessels were ordered back to Buffalo. General Scott, with his staff and a number of men, was aboard the *Sheldon Thompson*, captained by Augustus Walker. They were cholera-free until a couple of days out of Chicago, when one man suddenly sickened and died.

By the time the *Sheldon Thompson* dropped anchor off Chicago on July 10, 13 enlisted men had been lowered over the side. Three others died as the voyage ended. In a letter, Captain Walker adds a grim footnote:

Before landing the troops next morning, we were under the painful

Scott (1786-1866), whose nickname was "Old Fuss and Feathers," has been called the finest United States general after Washington and before Robert E. Lee. He served brilliantly during the War of 1812, the Indian campaigns, and the Mexican War. But as the Whig nominee for President in 1852, he was soundly beaten by Franklin Pierce.

necessity of committing three more to the deep, who died during the night. . . . These three were anchored to the bottom in two and a-half fathoms, the water being so clear that their forms could be clearly seen from our decks. This unwelcome sight created such excitement, working upon the superstitious fears of some of the crew, that prudence dictated that we weigh anchor and move a distance, sufficient to shut from sight a scene that seemed to haunt the imagination, and influence the mind.

The plague continued after the troops came ashore and replaced Whistler's men in the fort. Eighteen others died during the first day and night on land; their bodies, wrapped in blankets, were buried in a common grave at the corner of Lake Street and Wabash Avenue. Whistler's men, meanwhile, had set up tents. Most of the visiting settlers, fearing the plague even more than the thought of marauding Indians, had disappeared. So far as civilians went, Chicago was almost a ghost town.

By July 20, General Scott thought it prudent to leave with as many of his command as could travel. They camped near Riverside, at the Desplaines River, until they were well enough to move on. After a week or so, Scott and his troops began marching north, by easy stages, to engage Black Hawk. Instead, they had a further rendezvous with cholera at Beloit, Wisconsin, and never fired a shot. On August 2, Black Hawk's flag of truce was again ignored in Vernon County, Wisconsin, near the mouth of the Bad Axe River. A combined force of militia and Col. Zachary Scott's regulars wiped out almost his entire band, including noncombatants. Black Hawk himself was a prisoner for more than a year. The Indian threat—both real and imagined—had ended.

When General Scott's troops were mobile once more, they were ordered to return south to Fort Armstrong, at Rock Island, by way of the Rock River Valley. So impressed were the men with the beauties of the region that, as their enlistments were up, they spread word through the East about this lush and lovely land waiting to be settled.

The memory of Black Hawk is kept alive by the huge statue overlooking the Rock River near Rock Island. It was cast by the famed Lorado Taft (1860-1936), a native of Elmwood, Illinois, who also sculpted for the Horticultural Building at the World's Columbian Exposition and taught at the Chicago Art Institute.

Final Curtain: The last Indian treaty that concerned Chicago was signed September 26, 1833, by chiefs of the United Nation of the Chippewas, Ottawas, and Pottawatomies after a council that dragged on for more than a week. Once again, the Indians were forced to leave "for a land far toward the setting sun, which they had never seen and which they knew nothing of."

Terms of the "agreement" called for payments of $280,000 in 20 annual amounts of $14,000; $150,000 to build mills, shops, and other improvements on the home-to-be west of the Missouri; $20,000 for agricultural and other purposes; $65,000 in provisions, goods, and horses; and another $175,000 to a wildly assorted group of non-Indians with "claims" against the United Nation. Not surprisingly, Andreas notes that these applicants "were sufficiently numerous to constitute nearly a complete census of the white male population of the Northwest." His opinion of the $65,000 goods grant was equally harsh. One thing, however, was beyond doubt: "The Indian title to lands in Illinois was extinguished."

Although made half a century after the council, the judgments of Andreas echo those of an unbiased on-the-spot observer. He was Charles Joseph Latrobe, a 34-year-old travel writer from London, England, who reached "the little mushroom town" after six days on the road from Detroit. He missed the preliminary sparring, but was in time for the main event:

> The principal Commissioner [presumably Col. Owen] had opened it, as we learnt, by stating, that, as "the Great Father in Washington had heard that they wished to sell their land, he had sent the Commissioners to treat with them." The Indians promptly answered that . . . "their Great Father in Washington must have seen a bad bird which had told him a lie, for that far from wishing to sell their land, they wished to keep it." The Commissioner, nothing daunted, replied: "that nevertheless, as they had come together for a Council, they must take the matter into consideration. . . ." He then explained to them promptly the wishes of their Great Father, and asked their opinions thereon. Thus pressed, they looked at the sky, saw a few wandering clouds, and straightaway adjourned *sine die,* as the weather is not clear enough for so solemn a council.

Several thousand Indians watched the parley from an encampment across the river; they were a profitable market for traders who plied them with liquor. Latrobe describes the fort and the "half a hundred clapboard houses" which comprised Chicago at that time, then goes on to picture the "birds of passage," as he refers to the land speculators, grifters, sellers of food and other supplies, and those with real or fancied claims against the Indians, which they hoped to have paid by the commission's orders. The temporary Indian village, he says, was "in an uproar from morning to night, and from night to morning . . . [although] the whites seemed more pagan than the red men."

Latrobe's account of the event, which later appeared in his book *The Rambler in North America*, includes this scathing indictment of the commission: "It is a grievous thing that the Government is not strong-handed enough to put a stop to the shameful and scandalous sale of whiskey to those poor miserable

Several ships laden with whisky were prevented from reaching Chicago by contrary winds until the meeting had ended. This was much to the satisfaction of "temperance men, philanthropists, and Christians."

wretches. . . . Who will believe that any act, however formally executed by the chiefs, is valid as long as it is known that whiskey was one of the parties to the treaty.''

The frontier character of Chicago, a lively combination of ambition, high jinks, and let-tomorrow-look-after-itself, was about to change. The eccentrics and the color would remain but would be so outweighed by sobriety and calculation and drive to get ahead that they would hardly be noticed against the more pedestrian background. Still, this would take a few more years, and meanwhile . . .

Two Views: Colbee C. Benton, a visitor from New Hampshire, recorded these impressions prior to the September 1833 treaty-signing: ''The lots, many of them, are improved with temporary buildings, some not more than ten feet square, and they are scattered about like cattle on the prairie. . . . I believe there has been one hundred built this year, all without any regard to beauty, and they are set on blocks so that they can move them at the shortest notice.'' Benton found the inhabitants, who were ''living in all manner of ways,'' as odd as the buildings. One family had set up housekeeping on the main street, hanging their pot from a pole supported by two stakes.

Cleaver, the Englishman with the dogs, has left us a fine description of how time went by in Chicago just after it officially became a town.

''. . . And some good bird dogs'': Charles Cleaver, a Londoner, was one of Chicago's earliest citizens and never went home.

Checkers was a common game in the stores in the daytime, as well as in the evenings—as storekeepers had plenty of leisure while waiting for customers. . . .

Those religiously inclined went to prayer-meeting at least once a week. Then when boarders and travelers were satisfied as to the inner man in the old Sauganash Hotel, Mark Beaubien would bring out his fiddle and play for those who liked to trip the light fantastic toe. To be sure, there were no theatres, no concert-halls, or reading rooms. New York papers were twenty to thirty days old when we got them, and there were but few books in the place.

Cleaver's house, like many in the village, was unfinished, with only siding to afford protection from a temperature of 20 below. ''Fortunately we had warm clothing and would almost roast in front of a huge wood-fire . . . while our backs were covered with thick cloaks to keep from freezing. I actually had my cup freeze to the saucer while sitting at the table at breakfast. Stoves were not to be had.''

A Short History of Chicago

Although Chicago had been struggling to survive and prosper for roughly fifty years, its dwelling places were still lacking in comfort, much of their furnishings home-made. As the town reached the beginning stages of an organized community, there was even a shortage of food. Flour was going for $20 a barrel in 1833—when it could be found—and butter and potatoes were only a tantalizing memory. One of the few bright spots in a dreary winter was that navigation resumed early, and a small sloop, the *Westward Ho*, which had been confined in the river during the freezing months, was able to start regular trips to St. Joseph and bring back a dozen or so barrels of flour.

Shortages continued until the spring of 1834. In early May, a ship bearing flour and other provisions cheered the hearts of weary Chicagoans. The shipment went to George W. Dole, who for years was fondly remembered for his refusal to sell the flour for a proffered $25 a barrel. He said $10 was a fair enough price.

The last occasion on which Chicagoans saw Indians assembled in large numbers was when the Wisconsin Pottawatomies came for their final Illinois payment in 1835. There must have been mixed feelings among the whites—at least the more thoughtful of them. Certainly the Indians, who staged a frighteningly realistic war dance before calling it a day and trudging over the river bridge to head beyond Missouri, must have been wondering what birds they should listen to now.

Chicago—whose population now had passed 2,000—had fewer problems with the Indians gone. But the years to come would bring enough new and formidable ones to cause the rapidly dwindling band of "old settlers" to think wistfully from time to time of the early days and perhaps even long for their return. It is likely that the not-yet-old lady would have been among them, the one who would remark that "early Chicago was the happiest place in the world."

Young women were so scarce in Chicago during the thirties that it was the custom for the town's eligible bachelors to meet incoming vessels from Detroit or New York "ready to catch the girls as soon as they landed."

Roller Coaster Ride

4

The banishment of the Indians that suddenly made available vast enticements of fine Illinois land east of the Mississippi was also the signal for the newborn town of Chicago to begin a breakneck growth. More than 150 buildings—"houses, stores and shanties"—went up during 1834 along the line of the proposed Illinois and Michigan Canal, and the town limits were extended in February for the second time in three months. Chicago could boast of half a dozen lawyers, eight physicians, four religious denominations that held regular services (Methodist, Catholic, Presbyterian, and Baptist) and several hotels. There also were, Andreas adds, "A fair assortment of druggists, merchants, butchers, carpenters, blacksmiths and other artisans . . . [plus] a score of adventurers, comprising moneyed speculators and prospectors, as yet undecided whether to stay in Chicago or to go on."

Improvements to the harbor, a necessity if the canal was to be of any value, had begun in 1833 with the aid of a $25,000 federal grant. These continued, and the *Illinois*, the first schooner to enter the river, sailed all the way to Wolf Point on July 12, 1834, amidst wild celebration. There were even tentative efforts to fix the streets. Two were actually graded, and the town boldly borrowed $60 to pay for draining a large and stagnant pool of water on State Street.

More colorful events took place as well. The first murder trial was held, with an Irishman acquitted on a charge of killing his wife. A divorce suit, filed against a less impetuous husband, reached the courts in 1834, but the outcome is not known.

A carriage shop and the town's first bookstore opened, and the first professional paid entertainment was held in February 1834. Mr. Bowers, *Professeur de Tours Amusant*, gave an exhibition of ventriloquism, fire-eating, and legerdemain, "to begin at early candle-light" at the Mansion House on

Opposite page
The *Osceola*: The first ship to carry grain out of Chicago.

Street, admission 25 and 50 cents. Ventriloquism was popular. A second voice thrower, Mr. Kenworthy, arrived in June with his "entertaining monologue of the Bromback Family." In that same month the town borrowed $2,000 to use for improving sanitation in an effort to head off a threatened cholera epidemic.

A post road of sorts between Chicago and Milwaukee was improved during the year; trees were blazed to mark the route, bridges and boundary stakes put in, and some trees removed. A permanent Board of Health was established in 1835, and a Volunteer Fire Department organized—both desperately needed. After fire wardens were named, it became mandatory for all able-bodied male citizens to help fight a blaze when ordered to do so or be fined $2. The first fire engine was purchased in December, for $894.38 (payable in two annual installments) and the first engine company formed, the "Fire Kings."

By mid-April 1835 the vanguard of a huge throng of immigrants reached Chicago—perhaps lured by soldiers' tales and the banishment of the Indians. Within a month, Andreas observes, the town was swamped, with "no room for the constant crowd of incomers, except as buildings were hastily put up for the accommodation, or as sojourners, leaving the town, made room for them. The hotels and boarding houses were full, and full meant three in a bed sometimes, with the floor covered besides." Many of the new arrivals moved on after a brief stay to take up fertile acres further west, but enough remained so that the population climbed daily. A census taken in 1835 showed 3,265 permanent residents (including sailors on vessels whose home port was Chicago)—almost double the number a year earlier.

Land Fever: During the four-year period between its incorporation as a town and its becoming a city, Chicago was a center of unrestrained land speculation. The influx of settlers and the prospect of a canal had increased land values. This citywide gambling spree, when "men exchanged lots very much as boys swap jack-knives," was initiated by the sale of public school lands late in October 1833. The school fund swelled by $38,619.47 during the five-day auction of 140 square blocks of city land. The area sold covered roughly one square mile; the average price was $6.72 an acre, "quite beyond expectation."

As swarms of new arrivals reached Chicago, almost everyone in town came down with a severe case of land fever. Gurdon S. Hubbard—the former fur company employee, now a prominent businessman—and two partners bought 50 acres of North Side land for $5,000 in 1836. A few months later he peddled half of it in New York City for $80,000. Hubbard also was paid $80,000

Incredible as it may seem today, John S. C. Hogan, the city treasurer and former postmaster, resigned in protest against the city going into debt.

Early pastor: The Reverend Jeremiah Porter of the First Presbyterian Church married schoolteacher Chappel in 1835.

Hubbard was eventually to be owner of a sprawling packing plant of such proportions it would be known as "Hubbard's folly."

A Short History of Chicago

for the two lots he had bought in 1831 for less than $80.

Another wheeler dealer, John Stephen Wright, came to town with his parents in 1834 when he was only 19 years old and began dabbling in real estate. In 1835, while on a business trip to New York City with his father, he sold for $10,000 eighty acres in Chicago for which he had paid $4,000. A couple of years later, still using only his own resources, he had acquired title to property valued at $200,000.

It was not only along the canal route, or in Chicago, that land was so eagerly sought. "Paper" towns throughout the Northwest were plotted and sold, usually to buyers who never asked to see what they were buying. These towns were often located "wherever it was hoped a town might spring up."

For a graphic report on how land prices soared during the early years, it is hard to beat this account by J. D. Bonnell, who came to town in the mid-1830s.

> The most historic lot in Chicago undoubtedly is the one occupied by the Tremont House. It has been . . . swapped for ponies, refused for a barrel of whisky, and when an old settler wants to give you an idea of the city when he first stuck his brogans in the mud, he will somehow associate the price of the Tremont House lot with it. . . . One old codger will tell you, "When I came here I could have bought the lot the Tremont House stands on for a cord of wood." That means 1831. Another puts the value, with the preliminary remark, at a pair of boots. That means 1832. A third fixes the price at a barrel of whisky. That means 1833. A fourth adds a yoke of steers and a barrel of flour. That means 1834. A fifth talks about $500. That means 1835. A year or two afterward it was worth $5,000, and now [1867] it is nearer $500,000.

Harriet Martineau, an English writer who came to Chicago in 1836, found it the busiest place she had ever seen. The streets were crowded with men offering bargains in land "and a negro, dressed up in scarlet, bearing a scarlet flag, and riding a horse with housings of scarlet, . . . announced the time of the sales." But the cool-eyed visitor wasn't taken in. She predicted the speedy end of "this money-making evil" and a quick bursting of the bubble.

Warning Signs: Between 1832 and 1836, land sales soared from $2,362,000 to $24,877,000—much of it in paper unsecured by hard currency. A delinquent tax list, published in the *Chicago American* of October 1, 1836, was a feeble warning to the gamblers.

Despite the ominous signs, commerce was brisk in Chicago in most of 1836. Her businesses had combined sales totaling a million dollars, and between April 18 and the first of December, 49 steamers, 10 ships, 26 brigs, 363 schooners, and 8 sloops arrived. The Galena and Chicago Union Railroad was granted a charter in January 1836, although serious construction work wouldn't start for another 12 years.

But federal action, in particular President Andrew Jackson's Specie Circular of July 11, 1836, broke the balloon as well as a number of Western banks. Jackson's order provided that after August 15, with one minor exception, nothing but gold or silver could be used to buy public land, and that any bank refusing to redeem its paper money in specie would have its issues discredited and lose all further government business.

The young entrepreneur John Wright complained of the Jackson order, though rather merrily, as befitted a true Chicagoan. "I came to Chicago with nothing, failed for $100,000, and could have failed for a million if he had let the bubble burst in the natural way."

Most viewed the situation more somberly. The Panic of 1837, which came close on the heels of the Specie Circular, shook the whole nation. Chicago was especially hard hit. Land valued at $1,000 in 1833 was suddenly worth only $50—while the last speculator's note for the now worthless property remained at $1,000. In 1837, when the town became a city, "many of its inhabitants . . . were in sackcloth and ashes."

The Canal and the City: A temporarily hopeful event took place on the Fourth of July, 1836, when construction on the Illinois and Michigan Canal officially began. Hundreds of Chicagoans journeyed to Canalport (near Bridgeport) by boat, rode horseback or in carriages, or even walked to watch the first shovelful of dirt turned and listen to a big-gun salute and some long-winded speeches. There was a natural spring, too—spiked first with lemonade and later by something more potent. It all seemed a fine portent for continuing prosperity, although that prosperity was built on a foundation of paper.

Among the speakers was Judge Theophilus Smith of the Illinois Supreme Court. Smith mounted a barrel, read the Declaration of Independence, and spoke glowingly of Chicago's prospects. He predicted the city would have a population of 20,000 in another 20 years, and 50,000 in 50. This inspired one skeptical listener to inquire how big Chicago would be in 100 years.

"Yes, fellow citizens," Judge Smith shouted, "in a hundred years from this time you will have a city of 100,000!"

Fernando Jones, who was present, continues this story: "This was too much for the boys. They took him off the barrel and threw water in his face.

'Arrah,' said the leader, 'if we hadn't stopped you, you'd have made it a million.'"

In fact, when the town was granted its city charter on March 4, 1837, the population was almost stalled at 4,170. The election of city officers was held soon afterward, on the first Tuesday in May. There were only two candidates for mayor: William B. Ogden, 31 years old, a former New York State senator, and John H. Kinzie, 33, the eldest son of the late John Kinzie. The men, who were good friends, were both handsome, Episcopal, and well-liked. The poll list consisted mostly of names indicating an English or Eastern background, with a few French names and that of one Indian, Star Foot. Ogden won the election 469 to 237, with Star Foot voting for Kinzie, one of the best supporters the Indians ever had. Voting at the time was done "viva voce" with each person approaching the table where votes were recorded and announcing his choice for all to hear.

About two weeks after the election, the city—which began its existence with only $1,993 in the treasury—applied for a $25,000 loan from the local branch of the State Bank of Illinois. The money was needed for street drainage and the purchase of two new fire engines, but the request was turned down. The city thereupon issued scrip in denominations of $1, $2, and $3. The paper could be used to pay city taxes, up to $5,000, and carried interest of 1 percent.

Money was so tight in Chicago and the country at large by the summer of 1837 that many were urging the repudiation of both public and private debts—a stance which enraged the new mayor. Ogden, himself a heavy loser on land deals, addressed a mass meeting where he urged his fellow citizens "not to proclaim their own dishonor" and, above all, not to "tarnish the honor of our infant city." His plea in behalf of Chicago was heeded.

Chicago's first mayor: William B. Ogden also headed Rush Medical College and the Union Pacific Railroad.

No Business Like Show Business: Entertainment always has been a solace when times were hard, and there were several license applications during 1837 from showmen wishing to bring circuses or other spectacles to town. Most dropped negotiations when the City Council asked fees ranging from $100 for a year to $100 for a month (in the case of the New York Arena, which planned to display some "Natural and Artificial Curiosities together with acts of Horsemanship").

The first theater license was issued in October 1837 to Harry Isherwood and Alexander McKenzie, who took over the old Sauganash Hotel, vacated by the owners as they moved into a new United States Hotel on the west side of the river. The large dining room of the Sauganash, with seats and chairs installed, accommodated about 300 patrons, and admission was 75 cents.

The company included T. Sankey, old man; Mrs. Ingersoll, leading lady "and the best actress ever belonging to a Chicago stock company"; Mr. McKenzie, utility; Mrs. McKenzie, "a lady of rare ability"; and Master Burk, juvenile parts and fancy dancer.

Curtain-raiser: Harry Isherwood and partner opened Chicago's first theater in the Sauganash Hotel in 1837. He also painted the scenery.

Theatergoers who arrived about 7:30 would sit through a drama, a farce, and possibly a third offering, and watch the final curtain come down about midnight. The first season lasted six weeks or so after which the company went on tour; it was thought useless to stay open in Chicago during the winter.

In a letter to the theater owner, J. H. McVicker, in 1883, Isherwood described first arriving in Chicago at night "in a pelting rain." He arose the next morning to look at the town, and saw "a plank road, about three feet wide" in front of his hotel "and to my astonishment a flock of quail on the plank." He quickly decided not to risk playing the town, but the hotel proprietor gave him such a golden account of the prospects that he changed his mind. Isherwood remembered also that "a young Irishman who made one of the party, became very unruly and I was obliged to tell him to go. He replied: 'Where can I go, with Lake Michigan roaring on one side and the bloody prairie wolves roaring on the other?'"

Isherwood and McKenzie applied for another license in 1839, this time for what they hoped would be a permanent new theater, the Rialto, on the west side of Dearborn between Lake and South Water in the heart of the business district. The Tremont House and the Eagle were in the same block, and the Refectory, the city's only eating place, across the street.

The season in the new Chicago Theater, as the Rialto soon was renamed, was such a success that a committee of grateful citizens sent a glowing letter to McKenzie, the company manager. The high caliber of McKenzie's company persuaded many Chicagoans to accept the theater as respectable for the first time and set the stage—so to speak—for the city's subsequent role as a warm theater host.

The *Chicago American,* which began publication in 1835, treated theater as legitimate news. In an editorial on September 5, 1836 it asked, "Why do not the fair ladies of our city lend the theater, occasionally, the light of their countenance?" The *Chicago American* added that in Springfield plays were attended by "the beauty and fashion of the fair sex" and that the stage afforded "an innocent and instructive recreation." The newspaper reviewed later shows, and in writing of the September 14th performance of *Oliver Twist* remarked, "The front seats and boxes were lighted up with the beauty and smiles of the fair sex."

Stutter Step: The population decreased slightly, or remained the same, in 1838 and 1839, then resumed its steady climb. The first stagecoach did not enter the city until 1831, but by 1839 there were regular trips to Niles, Michigan (where the stage met the train for Detroit) as well as runs to Milwaukee, Galena, and other places. Steamboats also helped speed traffic heading north or east.

The first steamboat built in Chicago, the *James Allen*, was named in honor of the very popular young army engineer who had directed much of the harbor improvement work. Launched in 1838, it was soon making mail and excursion runs to St. Joe. These trips were often taken by the young men and women of the community, and Mark Beaubien seems to have been a regular attraction— if a couplet which has survived the years is indicative. The youthful passengers used to chant:

> Come, Uncle Mark, tune your old violin,
> And give us a dance on the James Al-*lin*.

As a contemporary account states, "The great steamboat line in the 1830s was from Buffalo to Chicago, about 1,000 miles, and a Chicago boat, with such men as Captains Blake and Appleby and others on deck, was looked upon as one of the great 'institutions' of the country. They were positively traveling luxuries."

The steamer herself, however, proved to be highly temperamental. On the trial run to St. Joe, she did the first 14 miles in under an hour. Then, apparently because her boilers were too small to maintain a constant head of steam, the *James Allen* managed to cover only about 7 miles an hour thereafter. According to her captain, "She would run like a skeered dog" for about half an hour, then invariably slow down. All efforts to remedy this quirk failed, and the *James Allen* was sold after two seasons.

The city's growth was evident in many ways. The first shipment of grain (78 bushels to Buffalo) was sent out in 1838; by the next year, 3,768 bushels were loaded from farmers' wagons onto the brig *Osceola* after being hoisted to the roof of the Newberry and Dole Warehouse and thence "piped" to the *Osceola*'s deck. People were so eager for culture that the new Young Men's Association of Chicago signed 150 members within a week at $2 apiece. There were enough buildings for a major fire; 18 structures including the Tremont House burned in 1839, with the damage estimated at $60,000.

The Young Men's Association established a reading room with newspapers and magazines above a barbershop at Lake and Clark streets. It had guest lecturers, soon was given a number of books, and eventually became the Chicago Library Association.

But despite these signs of progress, the young city had a frontier mentality. The public hanging on July 10, 1840, of John Stone, the first murderer convicted in Cook County, drew a lively crowd to the lakeshore three miles south of the Courthouse.

Stone, a 34-year-old Irishman, had been found guilty of raping and killing a Mrs. Lucretia Thompson. The account of his execution in the *Chicago American* says Stone maintained his innocence to the end. He asserted that two other men were guilty of the crimes while adding that "he would swing before their blood should be upon him." The writer mentions the large crowd, "among whom we regretted to see many women enjoying the sight."

In view of the circumstantial nature of the evidence, Stone's protestations would have carried more weight if his own character had been spotless. Unfortunately, he had been convicted in Canada for complicity in the robbery

Spectators at the hanging included about 200 citizens, 60 uniformed members of the state militia, and the Rev. Isaac W. Hallam, who read a brief service. Sheriff Gavin repeated Stone's parting statement aloud, and "seemed particularly affected, even unto tears."

The Know-Nothings, so-called because they professed ignorance when asked about their organization, were violently anti-Catholic and anti-immigrant.

and murder of a government officer, after which he fled to New York State—where he was jailed for stealing horses.

In the same month the *Chicago American* ran a paid advertisement petitioning Congress to disfranchise permanently all foreign-born residents of the United States not yet given the right to vote. This was signed by 250 Cook County residents, and was a kind of preview of the American or Know-Nothing party, which would come into brief prominence in the 1850s.

Fluted columns and a prairie schooner: The city's first courthouse, 1835, at Clark and Randolph streets.

Stormy Weather: Chicago faced a number of problems as it reached its fifth birthday as a city. The streets were either too dusty or too muddy, depending on the season, and provided many wry jests. The most-repeated, perhaps, was the tale of the man seemingly chest deep in mire on one

of the main thoroughfares calmly telling concerned bystanders not to worry "because I have a horse under me." Gustav Unonius, a Swedish immigrant who passed through in 1845, later recalled the city as a "vast mud puddle."

More serious was the fact that the city's up-and-down economy hit bottom once more when work on the canal halted for lack of funds in 1842. Municipal treasury orders were selling far below face value, and there were so many business failures that the District Court of Illinois held a special three-month session to hear bankruptcy cases only. "Practically all of the leading business men of 1836," Pierce has written, "were either bankrupt or greatly impoverished by 1842." The State Bank of Illinois began selling unpaid-for land; many canal workers were out of jobs and penniless, and there was an unprecedented number of houses to rent with no renters. Nonetheless, the population kept climbing.

The outlook soon brightened as Illinois obtained an additional $1,600,000 in canal loans from out-of-town sources, including New York, Boston, London, and Paris. Former mayor "Long John" Wentworth (who in 1843 became the youngest member of Congress and the first ever elected from Chicago) helped obtain the new capital, which permitted work on the canal to return to full swing by 1843.

Temperance reared its sober head, with four organizations of nondrinkers established by late 1843. Their total membership was 1,989 out of a population of 7,580. But the most critical problem was slavery, an issue which had been angrily debated in Chicago for several years. The city was already a center of antislavery agitation, and in 1843 many First Presbyterian parishioners who did not support the abolitionist cause founded the Second Presbyterian Church.

Wentworth's fame spread quickly. The *Cleveland Plain Dealer* once commented editorially that "Chicago is merely a windy place, where the principal productions are corner lots, statistics, and Long John Wentworth."

Abolitionism: Slavery was almost legalized in Illinois in 1824, and it was not until after the end of the Civil War that blacks were given equal status with whites under the law (if not in actuality). For decades before the infamous "Black Code" was repealed, blacks were forbidden by Illinois statute to testify in cases in which whites were either defendants or plaintiffs. Unless they could prove they were not escaped slaves, blacks could be imprisoned while being advertised as possible runaways. If "unclaimed" after a few weeks, prisoners were sold at auction to recover the costs of keeping them behind bars. They then had to serve their new masters with no more rights than if they were in the Deep South.

Possibly because of the severity and obvious injustice of the Black Code, there was ever-increasing support in Chicago for the abolition of slavery. Even among those who believed the South should do as it wished in its own area, many felt blacks heading for Canada and liberty should be helped when they reached free soil. Stories told by fugitives of life under the lash, and the occasional arrival of Southern law officers to reclaim fugitive "property" swelled abolitionist ranks.

The martyrdom of Elijah Lovejoy also created new antislavery sympathizers. The Reverend Lovejoy, one of the most dedicated abolitionists in the nation, had begun publishing his weekly *Observer* in St. Louis in 1833. His disturbingly articulate editorials brought many threats, and in 1836 he moved the paper to Alton, Illinois. Trouble and violence moved with him. An Alton mob smashed his press the moment it was brought ashore.

Fellow abolitionists—and others who simply believed in freedom of speech—raised money for a new press. But when Lovejoy urged the immediate abolition of slavery and suggested organizing an Anti-Slavery Society in Illinois, a second press was wrecked, and then a third. He was printing his heartfelt attacks on slavery on a fourth press when a mob stormed the paper's offices on November 7, 1837. Lovejoy was murdered, two days before his thirty-fifth birthday. The fatal assault was witnessed by Lovejoy's 24-year-old brother, the Rev. Owen Lovejoy, who inherited his brother's cause and his enemies.

Discord was widespread when an escaped slave named William "Box" Brown reached Chicago in 1836 or 1837 and quickly found friends. While awaiting arrangements for the final leg of his journey to Canada, Brown was the unannounced guest speaker at services of the First Methodist Episcopal Church at North Clark and Water streets. His speech created considerable excitement among a number of "proslavery Kentuckians" and others who didn't want church services disturbed. A group of protesters "buzzed around like bumble-bees, and finally put out the lights." Brown remained unperturbed, finished his talk, and things quieted down.

Another escaped slave was discovered near Lowell on the Vermilion River, La Salle County, one cold October morning in 1838. According to the abolitionist Zebina Eastman, he was "a most strange, famished, terrified negro, clad in rags and skins, and armed with a murderous looking knife extemporized from a scythe, and an equally rough looking gun, both of which he carefully guarded, evidently suspicious that they might be taken from him."

Four men living nearby decided to help the runaway despite the possibility of a $500 fine. These Scarlet Pimpernel types took the black to a farm whose owner "was a reader of the Bible and Roger's 'Herald of Freedom,'" and hid him in a barn. There he told his rescuers he had escaped from an Alabama plantation some time before, had reached Illinois, and had been jailed. He was

Philo Carpenter: Chicago's first druggist arrived in 1832, and helped organize the city's first antislavery meeting.

Brown's nickname derived from the fact that he had escaped from the South by hiding in a box.

Eastman, a dedicated abolitionist who edited *The Genius of Liberty* in 1841, was the first man known to have helped send a black to Canada by way of Chicago on the Underground Railroad.

A Short History of Chicago

then sold to pay expenses, and after serving some time with his new master, he had headed once more for Canada. The fugitive was taken by easy stages in farmers' wagons to Underground stations in Ottawa, Northville, Plainfield, Cass, and Lyons. At last he reached the home of Dr. Charles Volney Dyer, a Chicago abolitionist. A day or so later Dyer managed to get the man aboard the steamer *Illinois*, still carrying his gun and knife. Eastman reports:

> Captain Chelsey Blake, as usual, when several days out, made a tour of discovery to see what he might find on board, and among the firemen he found a "new hand," at which discovery he was very wroth, and made awful threats in a language more forcible than polite. However his fury ended by the positive determination to "kick him off the boat at the first port he came to." So as he came into the Detroit River, he made a grand circuit, as if to show off his fine boat to a circle of admiring Southerners on board, and ran it into a port on the Canadian shore, where he had no passengers to leave, but there he furiously dragged the negro from the lower regions and energetically "kicked him off" into freedom.

A Man for Sale: Chicago's earliest known antislavery meeting was a highly uneasy one held in semisecrecy soon after Lovejoy's death. To the relief of the organizers—mostly "professing Christians"—no mob attacked the hall. Eastman considers this gathering the start of the abolitionist feeling that was to bring the city fame for "sheltering and protecting the fugitive slave against illegal arrest."

The Chicago Anti-Slavery Society held its first public meeting on January 16, 1840, at the Saloon Building on Clark and Lake streets. Present were Ira Miltimore, an official of the Chicago Hydraulics Company, the Rev. Isaac T. Hinton, the Rev. Flavel Bascom, and other prominent Chicagoans. The resolutions passed included several favoring the peaceful abolition of slavery and repeal of the Black Code. On Christmas Day of that year, the *Chicago American* published a citizens' petition to the Illinois legislature asking that the black laws be erased. But another strange drama was to unfold before their final repeal in 1865.

In 1842 Edwin Heathcock, a black man, "industrious and well-behaved and a member of the Methodist church," was working as a laborer on the north branch of the river when he became embroiled in a noisy argument with a white fellow worker. The latter had him arrested for failure to possess the required proof-of-freedom paper. Heathcock was jailed for six weeks while his description was advertised along with a standard picture showing "a runaway

The federal census of 1850 showed that the city's population of 29,963 included 323 blacks.

"I've been in some big towns . . .": Chicago has the look of a metropolis in this view from the west in 1845. The population was 4,470 in 1840; 28,269 in 1850.

negro, bare-headed with a bundle held over his shoulder on a stick." Finally the newspapers carried an announcement that Heathcock would be sold to the highest bidder on Monday morning, November 14, near the log jail at La Salle and Randolph streets.

The Saturday evening before, however, Eastman, now publisher of the abolitionist *Western Citizen*, and Calvin DeWolf, a young law student and officer of the Chicago Anti-Slavery Society, met on Clark Street. They hurried to Eastman's print shop where they quickly ran off a number of handbills (headed "A MAN FOR SALE") which invited all citizens to attend the auction. These were posted all over the downtown area so that churchgoers would be sure to see them Sunday morning.

When sale time came, Sheriff S. J. Lowe, an Englishman and a man obviously embarrassed by the task, announced that according to law he was forced to sell the prisoner at auction. He called for bids. There were none. As

the crowd stood silently, Lowe warned that if Heathcock were not sold, he would be returned to jail and an auction held at a later date. At this point someone across the street called out: "I bid twenty-five cents!"

The bidder was Judge Mahlon D. Ogden, younger brother of former mayor William B. Ogden. Since Lowe could get no other bid, Ogden handed him a coin as the crowd cheered. Ogden then summoned Heathcock to him and said: "Edwin, I have bought you; I have given a quarter for you; you are now my man—my slave. Now, you go where you please."

Convict This Preacher: Like his brother, Owen Lovejoy was hated by many. In 1842 he went on trial in Bureau County Circuit Court on charges that he "did harbor, feed and aid" a fugitive slave called Nance. Published accounts of the trial are incomplete, but Lovejoy, who

John Dean Caton: Former Chief Justice Caton of the Illinois Supreme Court presided at the 1842 trial of Owen Lovejoy. Lovejoy was acquitted. Caton, incidentally, was an abolitionist.

served as his own defender with the aid of attorney James H. Collins of Chicago, was acquitted despite a "hostile jury" and the fact that one of his proslavery accusers approached State's Attorney B. F. Fridley before the trial and said: "Fridley, we want you to be sure and convict this preacher and send him to jail."

"Prison! Lovejoy to prison!" Fridley replied. "Your persecution will be a damned sight more likely to send him to Congress."

What helped Lovejoy the most, however, was that Nance's master talked a little too much. During his testimony he described taking her "from Kentucky to Missouri through Illinois." Lovejoy and Collins didn't miss this seemingly casual remark. Lovejoy promptly quoted some lines by Cowper:

Slaves cannot breathe in England, if their lungs
Receive our air, that *moment* they are free—
They *touch* our country, and their shackles fall!"

"And," Lovejoy added, "if this is the glory of England, is it not equally true of Illinois, her soil consecrated to freedom by the ordinance of 1787 and her own Constitution?" The presiding Supreme Court justice seemed to agree. In his charge to the jury, Judge John Dean Caton said that a slave brought voluntarily into a free state by his master thereby became free.

Attorney Collins contributed mightily to the outcome. He was one of the fiery band of Chicago abolitionists, and his closing speech lasted two days. Four years later he figured in a brilliant spur-of-the-moment defense of a slave who would have been returned to his owner in Missouri if Justice of the Peace Lewis C. Kercheval had issued an extradition order. Word of the proceedings spread quickly among antislavery Chicagoans, and Dr. Charles Dyer, a group of blacks, and "quite a number of respectable people" crowded into Kercheval's office. Since the fugitive had no lawyer, Collins was summoned. He looked over the papers and could find no legal reason to protest. But he was a great improviser. He calmly said, "This man is being charged with being a slave in Missouri. Now I deny that there is slavery in Missouri."

Amazed, Justice Kercheval retorted that everyone knew Missouri was a slave state. Collins was unmoved. "I deny it," he said, "and you can't take as evidence what everybody says; it must be proved before your honor. Your honor's court is of too high a grade to be taking evidence on hearsay."

Inquiry among the onlookers found no one who could swear, from his own knowledge, that there were slaves in Missouri. Justice Kercheval, not wishing to appear arbitrary or nonjudicial, ordered that a copy of the statutes of Missouri be found. By this time the crowd inside and outside the building was very large. While a messenger was sent in quest of the statutes, the prisoner became separated from the officer guarding him, and "somehow, like a bubble, glided over the heads of the throng and down the staircase to the sidewalk." The guard tried to follow without success, and the escaping black was "hoisted onto the highest seat of the best carriage on the street . . . and then driven by these daring young fellows down Lake Street to Lawyer Collins's office, while an immense crowd followed shouting and cheering." His rescuers took out a front window of the office; the fugitive stood on the sill, thanked them, and, it is presumed, became another of Dr. Dyer's Canada-bound "passengers."

There was an aftermath. Mayor John Chapin called a meeting in the Courthouse to determine ways to prevent mob action from giving Chicago a bad reputation. But before some prepared antiabolition resolutions could be presented, J. Young Scammon, a leading attorney and banker, put an end to the debate by proposing a series of rules to "prevent illegal arrests of people who had made Chicago an asylum from oppression."

Although this event marked the end of excitement under the Black Code, Chicagoans maintained their antislavery sentiments. In 1850, following passage of the notorious Fugitive Slave Act, the City Council resolved that Chicago police need not help recover runaways. The young city was to remain, in Andreas's words, "a hot-bed of abolitionism, where lived an uncompromising and undismayed set of radicals, whose strength was not to be despised."

A fellow attorney has described Collins as "a man of perseverance, pluck and resolution, and as combative as an English bulldog." Collins died of cholera in 1854.

Lincoln Is Chosen

5

There was a temporary halt in canal construction in 1847; the laborers struck for a 25-cent hourly raise and the hiring of a new foreman. Neither demand was granted, and work resumed after a two-week layoff. Employees in Chicago stores and brokerage houses had better luck. Their workday was cut to permit an early closing—8 P.M.! The city's first insane asylum, a private one managed by Dr. Edward Mead, was opened in 1845 on Kinzie Street but soon moved to a 20-acre site north of town. And a county hospital was started in old Tippecanoe Hall, on the southeast corner of Kinzie and State. It was run by doctors from Rush Medical College, which had opened in 1837.

Eighteen forty-seven also saw the opening of Cyrus H. McCormick's new reaper plant on the North Side, financed in part by money borrowed from William B. Ogden. There was a start, at long last, of work on the Galena and Chicago Union Railroad, and a fine new theater, the Rice, opened its doors.

All Eyes on Chicago: But the major event of 1847 was the chance to play host to the mammoth River and Harbor Convention. A huge tent was raised in Courthouse Square, and prominent persons attending included Horace Greeley, publisher of the *New York Tribune*, Thurlow Weed, editor of the *Evening Journal* of Albany, N.Y., Sen. Thomas Corwin of New York, Erastus Corning, president of the New York Central Railroad, and a newcomer to Congress from Illinois—Abraham Lincoln.

The convention was nonpolitical, planned by leading citizens of non-Southern states to focus national attention on the need for various waterway and harbor improvements. It was inspired in large part by President Polk's 1846 veto of a river and harbor bill and the contemptuous way in which he

Opposite page
Antietam battlefield: President Lincoln is shown with Gen. George McClellan and his staff.

referred to several of the 23 projects that the bill would have made possible. These "unimportant objects" (in the President's words) included river and harbor improvements at Chicago, Racine, Wisconsin, Little Fort (Waukegan), Illinois, and Milwaukee. The language of the veto drew a spluttering editorial in the *Chicago Journal* of August 12, 1846, which called it "an insult to the country," citing the millions "being squandered" by the North Carolinian Polk to invade Mexico and thereby extend slavery.

There was much recruiting nonetheless for the Mexican War in Chicago. So much enthusiasm erupted when the victory at the Battle of Buena Vista was announced in April that one luckless citizen lost an arm when a cannon went off prematurely during the celebration.

That others shared this view of Polk is obvious from a bit of doggerel written by James Russell Lowell in his *Biglow Papers*:

On'y look at the Demmercrats, see wat they've done
Jest simply by stickin' together like fun;
They've sucked us right into a mis'able war
Thet no one on earth ain't responsible for;
To the people they're allus ez slick ez molasses,
An' butter their bread on both sides The Masses,
Half of whom they've persuaded, by way of a joke,
Thet Washington's mantelpiece fell upon Polk.

When the three-day convention sessions opened on July 5 after a spectacular Fourth of July parade, it was by far the greatest gathering ever seen in the city. Chicago, with a population of about 16,000, found itself invaded by 20,000 visitors (of whom 3,000 were delegates from 18 states). Since no railroad had yet reached Chicago, most of the throng arrived by lake vessel.

In his Albany paper, Weed hailed the convention as the largest deliberative body ever held, predicting that Chicago would be as large as Albany in 10 years and that the city and its environs would have a population of 125,000 within 50 years. While there were no immediate results from the convention, its impact was felt on future sessions of Congress. The advertising received from the thousands who saw the city for the first time was of incalculable value in bringing Chicago new business and new residents. Essential to this expansion were the railroads and the Illinois and Michigan Canal.

Weather Clear, Track Fast: William B. Ogden and J. Young Scammon were the driving force behind the resurgent Galena and Chicago Union Railroad. They obtained funds from stock sold at various towns along the proposed right-of-way, from farmers eager for a faster method of shipping cattle and produce, and from lead miners in Galena. Even farm wives invested cash from the sale of butter, eggs, and cheese. (Oddly, there was considerable opposition to the line, principally from those with the same bias as the Marengo tavern keeper who declared that "railroads are undemocratic, aristocratic, institutions that would ride rough-shod over the people and grind them to powder. The only roads the people want are good common or plank-roads, upon which everyone can travel.")

By late autumn 1848, however, the young railroad was running from Chicago to the Desplaines River on secondhand "strap" rails purchased, with a used engine and a couple of passenger coaches, from the modernized Rochester and Tonawanda Railroad in New York State. The engine, promptly named the "Pioneer," and other equipment arrived on the brig *Buffalo* on October 10th. On October 20th a number of stockholders and newspaper editors took the 10-mile trip from the foot of Dearborn Street to the Desplaines. On the return journey, a farmer with a wagonload of wheat transferred it to the train, thus becoming the first man to ship on the Galena and Chicago Union. A week later there were 30 tons of grain waiting at the Desplaines terminal to be taken to Chicago.

The tracks were extended to Elgin by January 1850, and the 42.44 miles of right-of-way brought in $105,000 in freight and passenger revenue during an eleven-month period during which more than 37,000 persons were carried.

Plank roads proliferated just in time to be knocked out by the railroads. They were going north, south, and west as far as 50 miles from the city by 1854.

Linked at last: The railroad became Chicago's ticket to success.

The growth of the various railroad systems was phenomenal. In 1852 there was a noisy celebration as the first through passenger trains arrived from the East. The Michigan Southern train was greeted with such enthusiasm that "a salvo of artillery" was fired. The following year two speeding Michigan Southern and Michigan Central trains arrived at the Grand Junction crossing—at exactly the same time. Eighteen were killed in the crash, and 40 others brought to Chicago hospitals. The first rail connection between Chicago and the Mississippi was established soon after; on June 5, 1854, a Rock Island train brought 1,000 sightseers on a blue-ribbon excursion to the Gem of the Prairie.

When "the Illinois Central entered the field," says the invaluable Andreas, "trunk lines from all parts of the State and country commenced to stretch their giant arms toward Chicago." In 1847, he notes, Chicago had no railroads, and in 1848 the 10-mile track to the Desplaines River was laid. In 1855, however, there were 3,000 miles of "iron road"; by 1857 this had mushroomed to 4,000. Chicago was well on the way to becoming the nation's most important rail center, a transfer point for immigrants traveling west and northwest, and for goods heading everywhere.

> In June 1856 the first suburban trains began running out of Chicago. There were three trains daily to Hyde Park, a journey which can now be made in well under half an hour by automobile from downtown.

About the same time, the long dream of a direct water route from Chicago to New Orleans became a reality. On April 10, 1848, the *General Frye* was the first boat through the Illinois and Michigan Canal. It was towed from Lockport to the Chicago River, finally dropping anchor in Lake Michigan. The official opening of the canal came six days later, and boats left Chicago and La Salle simultaneously. The vessel from Chicago stopped in Lockport for another of the inevitable celebrations, but the *General Thornton* reached Chicago from La Salle April 24, and transferred to the steamer *Louisiana* sugar and other cargo loaded in New Orleans for Buffalo.

The completed link of the canal between Bridgeport and La Salle covered 96 miles and included 17 locks and 4 aqueducts. It was 60 feet wide at the surface, but only 6 feet deep (an economy measure). Freight was carried for 3½ cents a mile and passengers for 6 cents. The canal was a financial success for many years until the proliferation of railroads created too much competition.

> "It seems not to be generally known that, up to the time of the opening of the Illinois and Michigan Canal, Chicago was not at all troubled with mosquitoes; a blessing which amply compensated for many of our early deprivations."—John Wentworth.

With the canal completed, the town's attention turned to California and news of the Gold Rush of 1849. Guidebooks for the Far West sold briskly; wagon makers hired extra help and rushed into production designed for the long trek to the gold fields. Revolvers doubled in price, and Mackinac blankets and salt-cured food became almost impossible to find. In March the first of many parties started out for California. "The exodus thus begun continued throughout the year, carrying off many of the early citizens, whose names thereafter did not appear in the annals of Chicago," wrote one historian wistfully.

A Short History of Chicago

Death Comes by Ship: The influx of strangers by rail and boat from all parts of the nation was a mixed blessing. In the summer of 1849 cholera again reached Chicago aboard the steamer *John Drew*, which arrived with six already dead. Capt. John Pendleton died a few hours after bringing the ship in from New Orleans. There were no quarantine regulations governing arriving travelers at the time, and between July 23 and August 26, 1,000 Chicagoans fell ill and 314 died, 30 of them on August 1. In June 1854 a train pulled in with Norwegian immigrants bound for Wisconsin. Six were already dead from cholera, and a seventh died a few minutes after being carried from the train.

There had been a few apparently isolated cases of cholera a few months before, which the Health Department and newspapers had decided not to mention. But now there was no choice. Twenty other passengers from the death train were taken to City Hospital and put in quarantine. The disease spread very fast. In the first week of July, there were 242 deaths, and the rate continued at about 60 a day so that "the death cart was continually on the streets and the thoroughfares were crowded with hearses."

It was soon obvious that the treatment of those with cholera left something to be desired. Dr. Charles Dyer, the noted abolitionist, and other physicians were told that a steamer was arriving with 18 cases of cholera aboard. They met

Whimsical sidewalks: Up and down wooden walks such as these on Clark Street were a specialty in Chicago until the grade became more or less uniform.

the vessel and determined that half of those stricken had a good chance of recovery and the other half none. The 18 were taken to the hospital, where overworked doctors concentrated most of their efforts on the "lucky" 9—all of whom died. Those supposedly doomed, Dr. Dyer said ruefully, all survived.

Chicago could hardly have been classified as a healthy place to live, at least until a pure water supply, adequate drainage, and citywide sewers were available in the 1860s and 1870s. Between 1851 and 1855 there were 98 deaths from smallpox, 1,006 from "fever" (not otherwise classified), 1,220 from consumption, and 2,340 from cholera. In 1854, the worst year, 1,424 died from cholera alone.

Other improvements preceded those made for public health and made city life more pleasant, if not necessarily less risky. Gas-lit streets and buildings made their Chicago appearance at 2 P.M. on September 4, 1850. Both sides of Lake Street were illuminated "as far as the eye could see." The lamps were turned on again that evening, and several streets were lighted "in regular city style," according to the *Chicago Journal*, which added, "Some of the stores on Lake Street, particularly those devoted to California ware, made a brilliant appearance, and the gas lent an additional glory to refined gold. But the City Hall, with its thirty-six burners, is the brightest of all, night being transformed into mimic day."

Within a week or so, however, the City Council had ordered that no street lamps be lighted until citizens living nearby paid half the cost—$7.50 per lamp.

Between 1856 and 1858 the city's plans for raising the street grade went

Strange tender: Actually, $3 bills weren't uncommon in 1852.

A Short History of Chicago

ahead on schedule, despite protests from Lake Street building owners and a highly critical editorial in the *Chicago Tribune,* complaining that it would be necessary to raise every house in the city six or seven feet—or enter them through doors built in the second story.

Nonetheless, the work went on. The Tremont itself was lifted by workmen directed by George M. Pullman (newly arrived from New York), who used 2,500 jackscrews and 500 men to raise the five-story brick building eight feet—guests still inside—without inconveniencing anyone or so much as cracking a pane of glass!

The project, however, cost the Tremont's owners $45,000.

The task of elevating virtually the entire central portion of the city to the proper grade was completed by the late 1850s, thus ending the merriment among out-of-town visitors. One wag had suggested that New Orleans should quit worrying about its low terrain because he had seen a five-story brick hotel in Chicago that was so heavy it had sunk several feet into the ground.

Alarms and Amateurs: As the city remained halfway between its pioneer beginnings and its emergence into modernity, fire remained one of the most menacing and frequent happenings, and the year 1857 went out on a melancholy note. On October 19th the city's worst fire to date broke out in a four-story building occupied largely by "men and women of ill-fame" who were "indulging in a drunken carousal" according to the papers. One of them upset an oil lamp, the flames eventually took over other buildings, and, before they were extinguished, 13 people had died.

The coroner's inquest was told that the fire fighting had been hampered by the absence of two engines. These had broken down a week earlier while competing for a $200 silver trumpet offered as a prize at the county fair for the company that could throw a stream of water the greatest distance horizontally through 500 feet of hose. The two engines ruptured their air chambers during the competition, which was won by Engine Co. No. 7 (it threw a level stream of water more than 200 feet). A couple of other engines burst hoses during the contest, and 500 feet of hose was inadvertently left behind.

Tribute to the mayor: The "Long John," named for Mayor "Long John" Wentworth. It was the city's first permanent steam engine, bought in 1857 and still in service during the Great Fire of 1871.

There also was a major fire at the Holt and Mason lumberyard on Market Street January 26, 1858. This blaze got a firm foothold because the wrong alarm was sounded. The flames spread quickly, finally seizing a series of wooden structures nearby, and there was considerable concern that the conflagration might reach the gas works. A few days later it was discovered that the $100,000 fire had been set by a fireman nicknamed "Beast" Brown in revenge for the failure of the lumberyard owners to subscribe to the Firemen's Ball, sponsored by Engine Co. No. 4. Brown went to the penitentiary after implicating two

Signs of the times: Low-hanging awnings and signs were declared illegal in 1857 and Mayor Wentworth ordered police to gather them up in a nocturnal roundup. Those who paid fines were allowed to claim their property.

other men.

Criticism of the department was widespread by now. Engine Co. No. 4 ("Red Jacket") and Engine Co. No. 14 ("Red Rover") were particularly disliked. It was said that the men of No. 4 had burned down their own engine house in 1857, while the men of No. 14 had been stigmatized in a report by the Committee on Fire and Water in 1858 as "composed of a very inferior class of beings, all more or less being given to intoxication and guilty of rowdyism generally."

It apparently was because of this report, plus the silver trumpet and arson incidents, that the City Council voted in August 1858 for the creation of a paid fire department. The volunteer firemen (who disappeared completely by 1862) never had achieved a totally professional outlook. They raced each other to fires, fought company against company, and were not above drinking free whiskey while fighting a blaze.

The new department quickly obtained a number of steam engines to replace the older models. The first of these, named "Long John," was bought in the fall of 1857 (when Wentworth was still mayor) and went into service in February 1858.

Even after all of the firefighters were paid professionals, Chicago was plagued by a vast number of conflagrations. Between 1863 and 1872—omitting the Great Chicago Fire of 1871—3,697 fires did damage of $13,779,848, of which about $3 million was not covered by insurance.

The August ordinance also provided that only engines owned by the city could be used to fight fires. The volunteers had been buying their own.

Hopscotching Through the Fifties: Chicago changed rapidly during the fifties with much new building and civic improvement. There was a sharp growth in transportation facilities that would lead the city to become a center of commerce and shipping. Antislavery sentiment continued to grow, as did the feeling that conflict between the North and South was growing near. Meanwhile, however, the city provided its citizens with some typical Chicago-style entertainment.

In 1853 Seth Paine and his so-called Spiritual Bank (actually the Bank of the City of Chicago) not surprisingly went out of business. Paine and Ira Eddy, his partner, both were believers in spiritualism. Through a medium named Mrs. Herrick they took advice from the spirit of Alexander Hamilton when things became difficult. The bank refused to lend money to anyone who drank, smoked, or wanted the money to pay debts, gamble, become a usurer, or speculate in real estate. Interest on loans was not to exceed 6 percent per annum.

After a varied subsequent career, Paine died in 1871. Probably no one ever lost a penny dealing with him, but few ever said his bank was anything but strange, as strange, in fact, as the three-dollar notes it issued.

In 1854 Stephen Douglas, who had fallen out of favor with many of his supporters by backing the Kansas-Nebraska Bill passed by Congress, was balked for four hours in attempts to give a speech defending his actions. Chicagoans pelted him with eggs or rotten apples (bystanders differed) and might have attacked him more seriously, it was said, except that he was accompanied by burly friends and because he displayed no personal fear whatever.

Eighteen fifty-five saw the resounding defeat of a proposed state temperance act, but not before a band of German-Americans (presumably the town's heaviest beer drinkers) rioted against the arrest of 200 saloon keepers under

The Little Giant: Stephen A. Douglas, who lost the presidency to Lincoln, died of typhoid fever in 1861.

"Top hat, black tie, and tails": John Wentworth, one of Chicago's most dedicated citizens, as he appeared in his mid-fifties. "Long John" was six feet six—without the topper.

In earlier days, Chicago was also known as the Windy City (as well as the Garden City and the Gem of the Prairie, two nicknames that did not endure). One school says the name was derived from the often-present wind, the other that it stems from every Chicagoan's invariable habit of boasting about his home town. As to the first explanation, many of the nation's cities are windier than Chicago. The second is harder to argue against.

newly enforced Sunday closing laws. After shooting began, the militia was called out. In the following vote on the temperance act, pro–beer voters in Chicago outnumbered the drys by 4,093 to 2,784.

By 1857, Chicagoans who had been around during the city's 20-year existence must have been unhappy and bewildered by some of the changes. On March 3rd there was disorder at two polling places with one would-be voter killed and another wounded. April saw a unique not-guilty plea in Recorder's Court by the attorney for four blacks accused of stealing chickens. Said the lawyer: under terms of the Dred Scott decision, his clients were chattels, not individuals. They were without any rights recognized by white persons, and therefore they were not subject to the same laws. The judge disagreed.

On April 20th of that year, Mayor Wentworth, angered at the doings of the criminal element that occupied the Sands (a tumbledown area near McCormick's reaper factory) personally led the police in a raid during which nine buildings were demolished and six others—mostly brothels—burned. An unconfirmed rumor was that Wentworth cunningly arranged for a dogfight to be advertised in a nearby neighborhood, thus temporarily emptying the Sands of its tougher occupants.

Perhaps observers of these events would have agreed with Caroline Kirkland, whose article about the city appeared in the *Atlantic Monthly* for September 1858:

> To describe Chicago, one would need all the superlatives set in a row. Grandest, flattest,—muddiest, dustiest,—hottest, coldest,—wettest, driest, . . .—most elegant in architecture, meanest in hovel-propping,— wildest in speculation, most solid in value,—proudest in self-esteem,— loudest in self-disparagement,—most lavish, most grasping,—most public-spirited in some things, blindest and darkest on some points of highest interest.

This city of superlatives now was the most populous in the Northwest, having grown from 4,170 to about 93,000 in only two decades.

Meeting at the Wigwam: The Republican National Convention was scheduled for 1860, and Chicago began campaigning to become the host city many months before. Indianapolis and St. Louis were its two principal rivals, but Chicago had a definite advantage: Joseph Medill, special Washington correspondent for the *Chicago Tribune*, was not only lobbying for the nomination of Abraham Lincoln but was also boosting Chicago as a logical convention site.

"An unbridled shriek": This was the reaction to Lincoln's nomination at the Republican convention held at Chicago's new Wigwam.

Late in 1859 Chicago was chosen, chiefly because of its numerous hotels. A structure called the "Wigwam" was speedily erected at Lake and Market streets, near the site of the old Sauganash Hotel. It was a barnlike building with remarkably fine acoustics. An estimated 30,000 persons came to town for the event, swamping the hotels, good and bad, and overflowing into private homes and onto an occasional billiards table.

Although hotel rates ranged from only $1.50 to $2.50 a night for bed and board, there were complaints about overcharging, perhaps because the railroads offered special convention bargains. A round-trip ticket from Chicago to Buffalo, for example, was only $15. Straw polls taken on some of the incoming trains quickly showed Sen. William H. Seward of New York to be the overwhelming choice.

The convention opened at noon on Wednesday, May 16, 1860, with about 10,000 spectators jamming the Wigwam to cheer for their favorite candidates. Some 60 newspapermen and 465 delegates were on the platform, and another 20,000 or so spectators, unable to crowd inside, congregated around the Wigwam, absorbing bits of color and information from those going in and out.

Nominations came Thursday afternoon and were brief and lackluster. It was expected that the voting would begin almost immediately and be a formality, with Seward the easy winner. But here, according to William E. Barton in his *Life of Lincoln,* fate and a wily (or perhaps unthinking) delegate intervened. The tally sheets were late arriving from the printer. While the delegates impatiently awaited their delivery, one of them moved that the session be adjourned until the following morning. This was done, and an evening and night of behind-the-scenes maneuvering began. Just prior to the adjournment,

Things looked so unpromising for Lincoln that Horace Greeley of the *New York Tribune* filed a story predicting victory for Seward despite the fact that Greeley was a Lincoln supporter.

however, Judge David Davis of Bloomington, in charge of masterminding the attempt to gain the nomination for Lincoln, lost hope. He wired Lincoln at Springfield, asking whether he would accept a vice-presidential spot instead.

Seward's principal weakness was that he was considered too radical and too strongly antislavery. Several of the Northern states were hostile to him as well, and the Lincoln forces began to make deals, meanwhile pointing out that if nominated, Seward could not carry Pennsylvania, would probably lose both Indiana and New Jersey, and that Illinois was almost sure to vote for Stephen Douglas, the Democratic nominee. Davis and the others hammered at these points, made their deals, and offered implausible promises. Davis also ignored a wire from Lincoln telling him, "Make no contracts that will bind me." Davis simply shrugged and told the others, "Lincoln ain't here and don't know what we have to meet." He then offered a Cabinet post for Simon Cameron of Pennsylvania, the strongest of the other candidates, in return for Pennsylvania's votes on the third ballot.

On the first ballot Seward received 123½ votes, almost exactly 100 less than needed to win; Lincoln received 102 and Cameron 50½. The rest were scattered. Cameron then withdrew. Seward picked up only 11 votes on the second ballot while Lincoln added 79. And on the third, Lincoln had 231½ votes, one and one-half short of victory, as Pennsylvania dutifully fell into line. One of the Ohio delegates then rose and announced a shift of four votes to Lincoln, making him the Republican candidate for President.

Cannons on the roofs of the Wigwam and the Tremont House, the Lincoln headquarters, boomed to announce Lincoln's victory to the city at large, but it was the sound within the Wigwam that impressed those present to a remarkable degree. The *Chicago Tribune* story compared it to the yell that must have gone up when the walls of Jericho fell. Someone else remarked, "It wasn't a shout, it was more than a shout. It was an unbridled shriek, such as I never heard before or since. It was almost unearthly."

Lincoln was elected in the fall, and on the advice of Allan Pinkerton, the famous Chicago detective, slipped into Washington for his inauguration by a different route and at a different time than expected. The inauguration ceremonies were held March 4, and on April 12, Confederate guns opened fire on Fort Sumter. The Civil War had begun.

The City and the War: Chicagoans responded enthusiastically at first to the call for men. Col. Elmer E. Ellsworth, founder of the finest drill team the country had ever seen, was the first Union officer killed. He was shot by the owner of an Alexandria, Virginia, hotel as he was ripping down a

Whether there were counterfeit admission tickets printed overnight and handed to the "Wide-Awakes," as Lincoln's supporters were called, is debated by historians.

Lincoln received 172,161 votes in Illinois and Douglas 160,215. Despite the closeness of the popular vote, Lincoln received all of the state's 11 electoral votes.

Confederate flag. The dead Chicagoan was a close friend of Lincoln, who wept at the news.

Sen. Stephen Douglas also died—of typhoid—shortly after hostilities began. When Lincoln was elected, Douglas had immediately pledged full support to the president and had been working hard to persuade his fellow Democrats, in particular those in southern Illinois, to stand by the Union.

Chicago continued to support the war willingly during the early years. By July 1861 Illinois had mustered four times as many troops as could be trained and equipped for the moment. Although the Irish were considered antiblack and largely pro-Southern, James A. Mulligan and his Irish Brigade fought superbly at Lexington, Missouri. Other ethnic groups too proved highly patriotic. The Jews, a very small percentage of Chicago's residents, formed a military unit early in 1862. The city also indirectly helped the war effort because McCormick's reapers freed so many farm workers for the army. Secretary of War Edwin Stanton remarked that "without McCormick's invention, I feel the North could not win, that the Union would be dismembered."

But as the months went by, the fervor waned. The *Chicago Times* became so antiwar that Gen. Ambrose Burnside ordered troops to seize the plant on June 2, 1863. This brought the immediate formation of two hostile groups. One wanted to seize the *Chicago Tribune* in retaliation; the other was planning to defend it. A wire went to Lincoln, however, who ordered Burnside's action against the *Chicago Times* rescinded.

In August 1864 another national convention, this one Democratic, was held in the Wigwam. The popular Union general George B. McClellan became the presidential nominee.

So weary were even the Republicans of the conflict that, although Lincoln had been nominated as their candidate, there were private maneuvers to have a second Republican convention called in September in Cincinnati for the purpose of nominating someone else. But Union victories put an end to this talk, and Lincoln defeated McClellan handily, with 212 electoral votes to the general's 21 and a popular majority of about 400,000 out of 4 million votes cast.

Late in 1864 Lincoln sought 6,000 additional men from Chicago. The protests were so heated that Joseph Medill led a delegation to Washington in March 1865 to argue against the levy. Lincoln listened, then replied:

> Gentlemen, after Boston, Chicago has been the chief instrument in bringing this war upon the country. . . . It is you who are largely responsible for making blood flow as it has. You called for war until we had it. You called for Emancipation, and I have given it to you. Whatever you have asked you have had. Now you come here begging to be let off from the

call for men, which I have made to carry out the war you have demanded.
You ought to be ashamed of yourselves. . . . Go home, and raise your
6,000 extra men."

Medill and the committee were properly chastened. As he later told Ida M.
Tarbell, the Lincoln biographer: "We all got up and went out, and when the
door closed one of my colleagues said: 'Well, gentlemen, the old man is right.
Let us never say anything about this but go home and raise the men.' And we
did."

Robert E. Lee surrendered at Appomattox Courthouse in April 1865, and
Chicagoans turned the city streets into a giant revel with fireworks, parades,
cannon salutes, and bonfires. The joy turned to grief five days later when
Lincoln was fatally wounded by John Wilkes Booth while watching *Our American
Cousin* from a box in Ford's Theater.

Chicago paid its final tribute to the late president on May 2 after the
black-draped funeral train had crept slowly into the city over the Illinois
Central tracks paralleling the lakeshore. The casket was taken to the Courthouse as thousands trudged behind. It remained there until an estimated
125,000 persons had filed past. Then Lincoln was taken to Springfield for
burial.

Chicago Is on a Roll: When the war ended, Chicago was larger than
Cincinnati and closing rapidly on St. Louis. The city was in the midst of
a giant manufacturing boom, and Chicago drummers, as salesmen
then were known, were familiar figures in both big and little towns throughout
the Midwest. Department stores such as Field and Leiter, which had just
moved into new quarters, also conducted a wholesale business—often far
more lucrative than the retail—and had their own corps of drummers calling
on smaller merchants.

The new Field and Leiter store occupied a six-story structure at State and
Washington streets erected by Potter Palmer, who had bought up a vast
amount of State Street property and was busily turning that undistinguished
street into the city's outstanding business thoroughfare. Palmer already had
announced plans for a new hotel, the Palmer House, to go up near "the marble
palace," as the Field and Leiter store was known.

In 1863 the city's overall size had increased to 24 square miles, and during
1864 about 6,000 new buildings went up. By 1865, 18 square miles of Chicago
were covered with buildings of one kind or another. Although less than 15
years old, the Chicago Historical Society already boasted of a new "spacious

and perfectly fireproof" structure at Dearborn and Ontario, and the *Chicago Tribune*'s new home at Dearborn and Madison, built in 1869 at a cost of $250,000, was considered so perfectly fireproof that it was agreed insurance would be senseless.

New enterprises in the city included the Pullman Palace Car Company, which began in 1867. There also was a splendid theater, the Crosby Opera House, on State Street, the opening of which was delayed in April 1865 in deference to the dead President. Within a year or so, however, Uranus Crosby found himself so strapped for funds that he decided to have a public lottery of both the theater and some valuable paintings therein. After a long selling campaign the drawing was held and a winner announced but never seen or heard from except by written communications. Crosby retained his theater—the mysterious winner supposedly sold it back to him—and also, by chance, won several of the better paintings. The outcry was so great that Crosby left town for a spell.

The city's growing wealth had attracted a great number of very disreputable persons during the sixties. These included gamblers and their women (often the proprietors of bawdy houses); prostitutes in such profusion that the *Chicago Tribune* estimated there might be as many as two thousand "chippies" in town; thieves; confidence men; and young chaps eager to earn the bounty offered for anyone willing to enlist in the army. This price finally rose to $400 per enlistment, and could be earned several times—if the enlistee were careful—by disappearing and reenlisting under a different moniker.

Some of Chicago's many visitors called her "the wickedest city in the country." They may have been right. "Conley's Patch," at Franklin and Adams, was distinguished by such mythic figures as the "Bengal Tigress," a black woman of such heroic proportions that it took several police working together to persuade her to submit to arrest. Or there was, in a little better part of town, "Irish Mollie" Cosgriff. Mollie ran a house on Fourth Avenue and was the moll of George Trussell, a former bank bookkeeper who was half-owner of "Drexel," the best trotting horse in the nation. By 1864 Mollie and George had been best-of-friends for about ten years, and it was rumored that he was about to leave her. So one day, wearing what was later described as a "gorgeous white moire dress," Mollie went on a hunting trip. She found Trussell in a saloon in Hairtrigger Block, on Randolph west of State, and staged an early version of "Frankie and Johnny," weeping profusely as the gambler died.

Two weeks later at the new Chicago Driving Park, there was a hotly contested race between "General Butler," driven by William McKeever, the horse's owner, and "Cooley," with Bill Riley handling the reins. Each won two heats, and the runoff was taking place as dusk fell. Both disappeared around

the far turn, where visibility was bad, and when they reappeared "General Butler" was running without a driver. McKeever's body was found beside the track, with his head smashed either by a rock or a fence rail. No one ever claimed credit.

Christmas Day 1865 marked the opening of the sprawling Union Stockyards, several miles southwest of the center of the city. There were other civic improvements as well. The lake tunnel, which would bring pure water from a "crib" two miles out in the lake, was begun in 1864 and finished in 1867. Not only did this bring an increase in water usage of 3 million gallons daily, but Franc Wilkie, the newspaperman and humorist, maintained that it also was the cause of a problem affecting many families: "The cleansing properties of the new water are wonderful. Children whose faces have been washed in it have been lost and never found. Their mothers cannot recognize them. It is proposed to establish a place where lost children may be gathered, and where only the old water will be used in their ablutions. In time, it is expected that many young children, whom nobody knows, will be recognized by their parents."

Whatever you might say about the "Gem of the Prairie," it certainly had grown up since its gentle beginnings. And it certainly was never dull.

Opposite page
On the hoof: The Union Stockyards, largest in the world for many years, were Chicago's pride and despair. They brought the city wealth and provided employment; there were, however, grave problems, such as those attacked by Upton Sinclair in his novel *The Jungle* (1908). Before closing in 1971, the mile-square Stockyards complex included a hotel, bank, and a daily newspaper devoted to news of the packing world.

"Hot Time in the Old Town"

6

It was not exactly a vintage year, but Wilbur F. Storey, the irascible publisher of the *Chicago Times*, did his best to see that 1870 was a memorable one. Reputedly because he was not on friendly terms with Albert Crosby, now running the Opera House, Storey printed numerous attacks on *Blondes*, starring Lydia Thompson, playing that theater for a highly successful second season.

The production, believed to be the first burlesque show ever seen in Chicago, was called "immoral" by the *Chicago Times*, which also charged the buxom British beauties with being "scantily-clad" and with "capering lasciviously and uttering gross indecencies." A line in a brief editorial about "bawds in the Opera House" was too much for Miss Thompson. She and a fellow trouper waylaid Storey near his Wabash Avenue home one sunny afternoon and horsewhipped him. Damage to the publisher was minimal, but he was stung enough to have the pair arrested. The two were fined $100 after a trial that the *Chicago Tribune* covered in six-column, gleeful detail.

The fines were suspended, however. Three thousand spectators stormed the next performance of *Blondes* and gave Miss Thompson and the others a roaring welcome as they capered lasciviously onto the stage.

Baseball had its serious professional beginnings in Chicago the same year. A new team, soon christened the Chicago White Stockings, held its first practice game April 9 in Drexel Park on the lakefront against a group of amateur stars. Then the professionals went on tour. They crushed New Orleans 57 to 0 on May 5, and on May 13 scored an incredible 157 runs in Memphis (but did permit the Bluff City team to score one run of its own). In September, again on the road, the White Stockings beat the powerful Red Stockings of Cincinnati and came home to a civic welcome by a crowd said to number 100,000. A

Opposite page
Hot money: Safes opened too soon after the Fire had an unfortunate tendency to inhale fresh oxygen and cause undamaged paper money and documents to burn. This man is cooling his safe as a precaution.

testimonial dinner at the Briggs House followed.

Crosby's Opera House was dark during the summer to permit extensive refurbishing, and a somewhat more sedate attraction than Miss Thompson was scheduled for the October 9 reopening. Theodore Thomas and his excellent orchestra were to have begun a ten-day engagement on that Monday night. But the curtain never went up. The theater was no longer there . . .

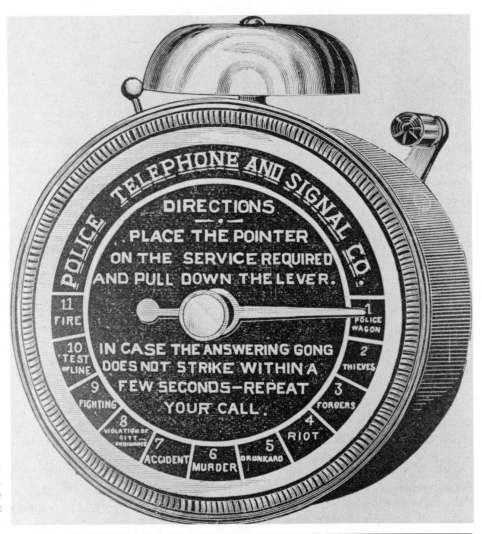

Dial-An-Emergency: Chicagoans had only to pull a handle after pointing the needle to the correct disaster.

Wooden City: In 1871 Chicago had about 300,000 residents, the vast majority of whom lived in wooden houses. The entire city, to exaggerate only slightly, was a huge potential bonfire waiting to be lit: There were wooden fences, wooden barns and outbuildings, wooden stables behind the wealthier homes—often containing a wooden carriage, hay, firewood, and oil. There were wooden warehouses bulging with inflammable items, lumber and coal yards, grain elevators, 55 miles of streets paved with pine blocks, a river jammed with wooden ships and spanned by wooden bridges, grass and trees dried to tinder-pitch, elevated sidewalks permitting a lively draft to spur flames along, and some fine buildings with wooden roofs so high above the street that the fire department hoses could not reach them.

The list of ingredients could go on: wooden railroad cars, huge complexes such as Cyrus McCormick's reaper plant, furniture warehouses, and varnish and paint factories.

Add that the rainfall between July and October was only one-fourth the average, with less than an inch falling during the previous month; remember that the fire department equipment was in poor repair because of a rash of recent fires, with hose in short supply and the firemen weary from overwork, and that many streets were blocked off near the river, thus preventing easy access to water.

Also, because even the biggest fires during the past few years always seemed to be extinguished before they could gobble up more than a few nearby buildings, the citizens had grown accustomed to the numerous alarms and to the warnings printed with increasing frequency in the daily papers. The *Tribune*, for example, was quite shrill as it described the city on September 1, 1871, as "miles of fire-traps, pleasing to the eye, looking substantial, but all sham and shingles. Walls have been run up a hundred feet high and but a single brick in thickness."

Shanties crowded up against substantial buildings in the business district, and some of the latter had wooden cornices painted to resemble metal or stone. Fire laws were not enforced. One estimate was that of the city's 60,000 buildings, more than 40,000 were fashioned completely of wood. Only a very few of the remainder were considered even remotely fireproof.

Dress Rehearsal: There was an eerie coincidence on the evening of October 7, when George Francis Train, nationally known world traveler and popular lecturer, spoke in Farwell Hall at Madison and Clark streets. For some reason, he declared that his talk would be the last one given in that auditorium. "A terrible calamity is impending over the city of Chicago," he said ominously. "More I cannot say; more I dare not utter."

It seems improbable that Train had a genuine premonition and much more likely that he glanced around the city during the afternoon, perhaps, and figured that a big fire *had* to break out soon. Only about 24 hours after he spoke in Farwell Hall, and an even shorter time after the *Chicago Times*, reporting his prophecy, had dubbed him "the Prince of Blatherskites," a very large fire erased about four blocks of Chicago in the area of Van Buren and Canal streets on the West Side. Several persons were hurt, and one housewife, home alone because of a badly swollen ankle, was burned to death when flames prevented her husband from reaching her.

The *Chicago Tribune*'s account of the disaster the following day echoed

"Mrs. O'Leary took a lantern to the shed": Except that when the fire broke out in the cow barn, Catherine O'Leary was fast asleep.

A Short History of Chicago

Train's warning in a more explicit and less mysterious fashion: "For days past alarm has followed alarm, but the comparatively trifling losses have familiarized us to the pealing Courthouse bell, and we had forgotten that the absence of rain for three weeks had left everything . . . in so dry and inflammable a condition that a spark might set a fire which would sweep from end to end of the city."

Discovered by a reporter in Denver a few weeks later, Train explained: "I knew that Chicago would be destroyed by fire or flood, and on the night in question I had a presentiment that a terrible doom was overhanging the city."

Sunday Punch: It was a warm Sunday evening on the eighth of October, and a one-legged drayman, Daniel Sullivan, known to his familiars as "Pegleg," was sitting across the street from the home of Patrick and Catherine O'Leary on DeKoven, a small cottage on the West Side that O'Leary bought in 1864 for $400. Sullivan was listening to the singing and laughter from a second tiny cottage on the same lot, which was rented from the O'Learys by a railroad man, Patrick McLaughlin. The McLaughlins were having a party in honor of Mrs. McLaughlin's brother, recently arrived from Ireland.

Sullivan sat on the wooden sidewalk, resting against the wooden fence, enjoying the balmy air, when shortly before 9 o'clock he saw a small finger of flame poke its way out of the O'Leary cow barn. He got to his foot and scrambled across the street as quickly as he could, hurrying to the barn as he yelled the alarm. He managed to rescue a half-grown calf, although he almost fell when his pegleg slipped on the board floor. Then the neighborhood, including the sleeping O'Learys, came awake.

By now the barn was briskly ablaze. The company in charge of the "America" hose cart, alerted by a nearby resident, was the first to reach the scene. They were soon joined by the "Little Giant" engine company, whose own lookout had spotted the flames. Meanwhile, a neighbor ran to a drugstore to turn in an alarm.

On first noticing the fire, the Courthouse watchman, Mathias Schafer, thought it was simply the reflection against some low-lying clouds of the West Side gas works, a phenomenon that had fooled him before. When he realized his mistake, he ordered the wrong box struck because the still-burning coal piles from the recent fire were on the same line as the O'Leary barn and made a quick judgment of the location very difficult.

Schafer then looked through his spyglass and immediately called down the speaking tube to William J. Brown, the fire alarm operator, telling him to strike a different box. The operator, busy eating his supper and chatting with his sister and her girl friend, refused, later explaining that he thought both boxes were in the same area and he felt this would be confusing. So Brown struck the same box again.

As a result the city's two newest steam engines, the "J. B. Rice" and the "R. A. Williams," failed to engage the fire until many minutes after they should have. By the time the errors were resolved and a number of engines and hose carts were fighting to bring the fire under control, the wind, strong but fitful, had begun scattering the flames and driving bits of blazing debris over a wide area. Several homes on Taylor Street, a block north of DeKoven, were burning, and the heat had become so intense that one fireman's leather hat was warped and his clothing began smoking.

Marshal Robert A. Williams, whose speed in reaching the scene of action was legendary, was already directing operations with the help of his deputy marshals. For a brief time, it seemed that the fire might be contained in the area of DeKoven, Taylor, and Jefferson streets, partly because the previous night's conflagration had created a kind of neutral zone that might serve as a firebreak.

The firemen fought like true professionals, sometimes remaining at a key spot until they were in danger of death. Some equipment had to be abandoned to the flames; hoses burst, and men were overcome, but still they fought.

Deputy Marshal Mathias Benner had been working on the second floor of the Turner Block, five two-story buildings on the east side of Jefferson just above DeKoven, ripping down ceilings so that water could be directed under the roof. He finally came down into the street where he met John Schank, the first assistant marshal, who told him to order as many engines as he could spare to the north. "John," Benner asked in astonishment, "where has the fire gone to?"

"She has gone to hell and gone," Schank replied.

Out of Control: Hope still lingered that the flames might be beaten until a wind blown brand found the roof of St. Paul's Church, about five blocks north of DeKoven. Several attempts to drown the resultant fire failed, in part because a ladder used to bring water close enough to reach the roof fell and broke. A short time after a devout Irish lady in the crowd of spectators said firmly, "God will put it out!" the roof fell in. Moments later the two Bateham's lumber mills behind St. Paul's were irrevocably ablaze, and shortly before midnight a fireman, running toward the "Long John" with a needed length of hose on his shoulder, encountered Marshal Williams and shouted: "Robert! The fire is on the South Side!"

Frantic householders and businessmen whose buildings were in the probable path of the advancing fire were emptying homes and stores of their contents and piling these in the middle of the streets. This salvaged property often began blazing, providing a fiery bridge.

A Short History of Chicago

Chicago in flames: The city burned for almost 24 hours.

Before the exhausted firemen had a real chance to gain any sort of edge, the flames began leap-frogging from building to building and dancing from street to street. Soon both the West and South sides were blanketed by a swirling mass of smoke, wind, and fire. The wind, which fed on itself and the ever-increasing heat, had reached incredible proportions. As Thomas Byrne of Hose Elevator No. 2 remembered later, "You couldn't see anything over you but fire. . . . No clouds, no stars, nothing but fire."

One indication of the extreme strength of the wind was that the Crib, two miles offshore in Lake Michigan, was menaced by a storm of burning debris that came sailing out of the night about 11 o'clock. John Tolland, the Crib keeper, sent his frightened wife to bed when the fiery barrage began, and using a broom and endless pails of water from the lake, fought ceaselessly until 4 o'clock Monday morning before he finally felt safe. He later admitted that between 2 and 3 A.M., the scarlet storm was so heavy that "I would have sold out my chances for a dollar to any man that came along."

Everything was tried to slow down the fire's advance, including blowing up or tearing down buildings to isolate it. But when some of the most substantial structures on the South Side began to go, including the Courthouse, the Sherman House, the Tremont (for the third time), the about-to-open Grand

Everyone afterward mentioned the wind, which finally developed demonic force. In the downtown section, at about the time the fire developed a foothold there shortly before midnight, an anemometer registered its force at 60 miles an hour.

"Hot Time in the Old Town"

Once known as: The Grand
Pacific Hotel.

A Short History of Chicago

Pacific, and even such a supposedly fireproof building as the *Chicago Tribune's*, it was obvious that virtually the entire city except for the far West and South sides was doomed.

Residents of the North Side, feeling at first that the river would prove an impassable barrier, were soon in flight. Superior Judge Joseph Easton Gary, whose brick home was on Ontario Street, announced early Monday morning that the fire would never reach that far and sternly ordered his daughters to stop packing for departure. Only when the windowsills started burning did the judge and his family leave, and by that time it was possible to go only in one direction—east to the lake.

As people fled, there were many strange and touching incidents. Odd things were saved: a rooster riding on the shoulder of its owner, four puppies cared for by a barefoot little girl, a fireplace mantel, a pack of playing cards, a stovepipe, an empty box, a feather duster, and the wooden Indian who found himself being wheeled away from the flames. One kind-hearted citizen saved two horses tied outside a Parmalee livery stable when they were threatened by fire, then spent several hours leading them to safety instead of saving the stock from his Lake Street store. He later advertised the horses and discovered they had belonged to the "Long John" engine, whose crew pulled it by hand after the horses vanished.

The excitement affected some in peculiar ways. A clothing store owner living on Third Avenue between Van Buren and Harrison began to take down his crystal chandeliers, then stopped to fire a revolver from an open window at the approaching flames. And a 14-year-old youth on Cass Street lingered behind his fleeing parents to fulfill a long-felt desire with a shotgun blast into a pair of matching French mirrors.

Shortly before the Courthouse bell came plummeting to the basement at 2:30 A.M., about 100 prisoners were freed from their cells in the building. The murderers were marched away under guard; the rest were simply turned loose, and many were given a gift: gems from the Miller jewelry store across the street that the jeweler himself was unable to carry away.

The fire reached the waterworks about 3 A.M. Monday, hitchhiking on a burning beam that came rocketing in and landed on the roof. In less than an hour the roof collapsed, and the waterworks was out of business. The only water remaining for the firemen—other than lake and river—was the limited amount in the mains. When the mains went dry, about 4:30 A.M., many of the fire fighters headed for home—or someplace.

Marshal Williams kept fighting with what weapons were left, drawing water from the lake and river where possible. The "Chicago," aided by a group of volunteers, saved the Lind Block at Randolph and the river, the only

Burnt district: The Fire took a great bite from the young city.

A woman driving the family wagon loaded with furniture met a neighbor and excitedly inquired, "Is this the Day of Judgment?" "Can't say," replied the neighbor, a Mr. Calhoun and presumably a New Englander. "No time for conundrums."

building standing in the business section after the flames swept through.

Finally, as the wind died down and scattered showers began falling about 11 P.M. Monday, the danger to what was left of the Gem of the Prairie seemed ended. Coal piles throughout the city smoldered for days, but the Great Chicago Fire was officially over.

The toll was a grievous one: while only about 120 bodies ever were found, as many as 250 to 300 persons may have died, some of them lost in the river and some completely consumed. The burned-out section was about a mile wide and four miles deep. Some 100,000 Chicagoans were homeless, and 17,500 buildings, shacks, mansions, great hotels, railroad depots, and business establishments such as Field and Leiter's "marble palace" or the shops of Booksellers' Row were gone. Financial losses were so great—about $250 million—that a number of insurance companies were unable to pay off.

Full Speed Ahead: One of the most impressive things after the fire was the speed with which Chicago moved into a business-as-usual posture. Margaret O'Toole, who sold chestnuts, was at her regular stand on Lake Street Tuesday morning, although customers were few. And an onlooker reported that at the same time the *Chicago Tribune* building was burning, a man was testing the bricks in the debris of the nearby Reynolds Block to see whether they had cooled enough to be used in rebuilding.

The last telegram sent from the Western Union office early Monday, before the fire drove everyone out, was cut off abruptly. It read: "The block immediately across the street from the telegraph office, one of the finest . . ." And among the early messages filed when telegraph service was restored was from a Chicagoan to his wife, temporarily in New York City: "Store and contents, dwelling and everything lost. Insurance worthless. See ——— ——— immediately; tell him to buy all the coffee he can and ship it this afternoon by express. Don't cry."

Western Union was back in business Tuesday morning, in a brick warehouse at State and 16th streets. Boards laid over barrels were the desks, and customers in a block-and-a-half-long line stood in the street, using the elevated sidewalks for writing tables as they waited.

Perhaps the most memorable sign to come down through the years was the one scrawled above a jerry-built shanty put up by William Kerfoot, a real estate man: "All gone but wife, children and energy."

The former home of Woods Museum was nothing but a pile of jagged rubble, yet it sported a notice on top: "COL. WOODS' MUSEUM—Standing Room Only, R. Marsh, Treasurer." Carl Pretzel, who put out a humor maga-

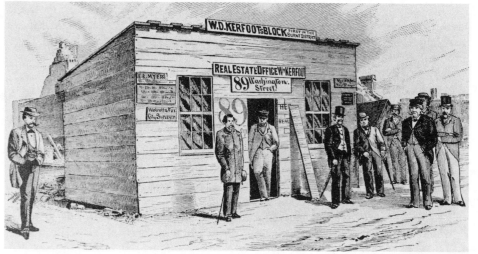

W.D. Kerfoot's block: The small print boasts "First in the Burnt District." Kerfoot gained immortality with an earlier sign "All gone but wife, children, and energy."

zine written in dialect, left a notation on what remained of his office: "Carl Pretzel, gon avay."

Those who resumed business without taking time to draw a reassuring breath included Field and Leiter, who managed to save some $600,000 worth of goods and haul it to a South Side stable that became their new store, and Moore and Goes, sign painters. They moved west, and the placard giving their new address had this information appended: "Capital, $000,000.30."

The *Chicago Tribune* and the other newspapers resumed publication in an amazingly short time. William Bross and Medill rented a small printing shop beyond the western limits of the fire. Bross located four stoves in a store on Halsted Street for which the owner insisted on cash—$16 each. Then he began looking for some place to raise the money. He finally found an acquaintance from whom he borrowed $60. The sign identifying the new *Chicago Tribune* building was painted by a man who said he had no money to feed his wife and children. He was paid $3.75 for the job.

The *Chicago Journal* moved in next door and shared the facilities, consisting largely of a hand press and a jumbled assortment of type. Tuesday afternoon the *Chicago Journal* got out an extra—printed on one side only and measuring four by six inches. Col. H. W. Farrar of the *Chicago Journal* had left for Cincinnati before the fire was over, to buy a rotary press. Medill heard of one for sale in Baltimore and bought it by phone. The *Chicago Tribune* requested dimensions by wire so that the foundation could be built while the press was being shipped. In the interim, Murat Halstead of the *Cincinnati Commercial* had found and sent a variety of old type to his friend, Medill.

Sign painting was one of the skills most in demand, although those engaging in it seem sometimes to have been in a hurry. One sign for a shoe store read: "SHOOES."

Only Wilbur Storey of the *Chicago Times* seemed overcome by despair, saying mournfully: "The *Chicago Times* is dead. Chicago is gone, and I'm all through." He then borrowed money, found some type, and the *Chicago Times* had an edition on the street by October 18.

Help from Everywhere: Food, clothing, and other supplies, including huge gifts of money, began pouring in from all over the world. New York City sent wagons through the streets collecting clothing, and special trains were on the way to Chicago in hours. Cincinnati raised $160,000 before sunset Monday, and Gov. John Palmer of Illinois sent three carloads of food and clothing the same day after calling a special session of the legislature to appropriate money for the stricken city.

Relief agencies were set up in many Chicago churches, and only a single complaint survives: the pastor of one of the city's burned-out churches asked for better-than-average supplies because of his "high-class parishioners." Before sunset Tuesday more than 50 carloads of food and clothing came rolling into the city. Milwaukee made a special effort to raise supplies (closing its schools for the day), while many businessmen went soliciting for Chicago rather than going to their offices. St. Louis, a bitter rival, sent a relief train the day after the fire.

President Grant sent $1,000 of his own money. A hundred mattresses came from the Cincinnati Elastic Sponge Mattress Company. The Jane Coombs Comedy Company turned over its box office receipts for one performance. The crew of the U.S.S. *Vermont* gave a day's pay, and a number of police departments, including those of Quebec and Louisville, offered funds earmarked for Chicago policemen. One of the most touching gifts was two days' pay from the newsboys of Cincinnati.

The final money total was $4,820,148.16, of which $973,897.80 came from 29 foreign countries. Furth, Bavaria, a manufacturing community, raised $2,302.31. The Common Council of London, England, voted a gift of 1,000 guineas while American cities responded with equal generosity: Boston gave $400,000, Buffalo gave $100,000, Lafayette, Indiana, donated $10,000, and New York City, $600,000. There also was $90 from the citizens of the Dakotah Territory.

Some of the donations were bizarre, to say the least. The Ohio Female College had a fine idea: 60 complete suits of ladies' undergarments. But what of the donors who forwarded stage costumes, brocaded silk dresses, white vests, lavender gloves, or fancy ball gowns?

There were unusually thoughtful gifts as well. Thomas Hughes, English

A Short History of Chicago

author of *Tom Brown's School Days*, began a drive for books for a Chicago city library. Among those responding were Queen Victoria, Charles Kingsley, John Stuart Mill, Dante Gabriel Rossetti, and Benjamin Disraeli, the novelist and former prime minister. Also received—and much appreciated—were 600 boxes of burn ointment and 16 dozen packages of Shield's eyewash.

Immediately behind the relief trains came freight cars packed with goods to restock Chicago stores and warehouses. Numerous offers of virtually unlimited credit also were forthcoming, and the city of Cincinnati opened and ran a soup kitchen at Green and Carroll streets that fed about 3,500 daily and was still serving food two months after the fire.

Out-of-towners wishing to help made personal visits. A relief group from Boston took the 55½-hour train ride to offer its services. The proprietor of the Townsend House in Oconomowoc, Wisconsin, arrived on Wednesday and asked the *Chicago Journal* to publicize his offer of free rooms for an indefinite period to former patrons or their friends. There also was a communication from a man in Curlew, Nebraska, offering free lots and cheap lumber ($16 a thousand feet) to any Chicagoans wishing to build new homes in Curlew.

Greed, Honesty and Oddballs: Prices skyrocketed after the fire, some legitimately, some through greed. The cost of meat and sugar doubled, and pure lake water went as high as $5 a barrel. Those who couldn't afford that drank water from the river, and typhoid broke out. When waterworks resumed operations October 27, the city's health improved.

There were honest folk, of course, including Pat O'Connell, a West Side grocer who offered free meat to anyone unable to pay, and W. K. Nixon, owner of a new South Division building, who cut rents 10 percent—even for those with leases already signed. But chiselers tried to take advantage of the postfire generosity. Non-Chicagoans attempted to get the free railroad passes offered those who were burned out, and some visitors to other cities posed as fire sufferers to obtain money. One of the Philadelphia papers commented on this: "Chicago was probably the most populous city in the world, previous to the conflagration. Some 14,000,000 of her 'destitute citizens' have passed through the city in the past three weeks. You can't throw a cat in any direction without hitting a 'sufferer.' "

Most of the reaction to Chicago's disastrous fire was one of pity and a desire to help. But some felt it was a heavenly reprisal for various sins. A Cincinnati clergyman and the Sons of Temperance from Urbana, Illinois, both expressed belief that the fire was an answer to Chicago's failure to close its saloons on Sunday. The Rushville, Indiana, *Democrat* suggested that the fire

The conflagration became such an obsessive conversation topic for survivors that a Boston newspaper editor said he would "give $500 to any Chicago man, woman, or child who can talk 10 minutes without mentioning the Great Fire."

The ashes: After the embers cooled, recovery seemed a distant prize.

In fact, the only nonaccidental death—other than two or three suicides—was that of a respected citizen coming home after curfew. He was shot and killed by one of Sheridan's college-boy militiamen in a tragic mixup.

was a divine repayment for General Sherman burning Atlanta, adding, "God adjusts balances. Maybe with Chicago the books are now squared." The *Chicago Times* carried a preposterous account of a group called the "Société Internationale," an anarchist organization that supposedly not only set the fire but also kept it going. There was a theory that a fire extinguisher salesman burned the town in anger over its poor response to his sales pitch, while the *Chicago Times,* perhaps having second thoughts about the anarchist yarn, speculated that Mrs. O'Leary burned her own barn after being dropped from the relief rolls as revenge against a city "that would deny her a bit of wood or a pound of bacon." The principal trouble with this was that not only was Mrs. O'Leary asleep when the fire began, but she never had been on relief.

Tales of incendiarism and looting were widely printed with convincing details about the lynching or shooting of the perpetrators. This seems to have been a case of too much imagination playing with a complete lack of facts. Lt. Gen. Philip Sheridan, who was asked to govern the city for a few days after Mayor Bowen declared martial law, said in his report that there were no known cases of arson or of anyone being killed by mobs. The crime rate, however, soared in the weeks after the fire. There was an influx of criminals and professional gamblers who thought that Chicago had suddenly become a wide-open frontier town. Homeless and penniless Chicagoans also turned to

A Short History of Chicago

theft as a means of getting by.

In an editorial in the *Chicago Tribune* three days after the fire, Joseph Medill proved to be an enthusiastic and accurate prophet when he said:

> All is not lost. Though four hundred million dollars worth of property has been destroyed, Chicago still exists. She was not a mere collection of stones, and bricks, and lumber . . . the lake, with its navies, the spacious harbor, the vast empire of production extending westward to the Pacific . . . the great arteries of trade and commerce, all remain unimpaired and undiminished, and all ready for immediate resumption. . . .
>
> We have lost money, but we have saved life, health, vigor and industry . . . let the Watchword henceforth be: *Chicago Shall Rise Again!*

It was no particular surprise the following month when Medill, running on the Fireproof ticket, was elected mayor of a city that already was well along with a world-class comeback.

One question undoubtedly never will be answered—how the fire began. The starting place has been established without doubt as the O'Leary barn. But the story that circulated immediately, blaming a cow for kicking over a lantern and burning the town, has long been discounted. Spontaneous combustion of hay stored in the barn, someone carelessly flipping a lighted cigar as he strolled through the alley, or other fanciful tales have been offered, but no proof given. Mrs. O'Leary, interviewed by a reporter, summed up the impact of the event as well as anyone could. The newspaperman asked whether the fire had been "rough" on her. "Rough!" she replied, with perhaps a faint touch of proprietary pride, "Why, my God, man, it was a terror to the world!"

One of the key figures in Chicago's swift renewal may have been banker Chauncy Blair, who nixed a proposal to pay depositors 25 cents on the dollar by saying: "If a dollar is found in the vaults of the Merchants' National when they are reached and opened, that dollar goes to the depositors."

Phoenix—Chicago Style! 7

Few fairy godmothers could have recreated a city faster or with greater confidence than Chicago rebuilt herself after the fire.

Nineteen national banks and 9 state and private ones were destroyed. But only 48 hours after the rains began falling, 12 already were established in temporary quarters, and so swiftly did new buildings of every sort appear that by October 1872, there were an estimated $34 million worth already up on the South Side, almost $4 million on the North Side, and close to $2 million on the least-damaged West Side.

The McVicker's Theater was open once more, hotels reappeared, newspapers were rebuilding their plants, and some department stores already were properly housed again. There was a new Courthouse/City Hall rising against the sky, as were dozens of churches, the Chicago Historical Society, and too many other factories, warehouses, and private dwellings to mention. There were improved building codes and safety laws, too—some of them obeyed. Wooden structures were forbidden in the business section.

There was also a new feeling abroad among the working men, who for many years had accepted what they were given—or not given—with passive resignation. In the mid-seventies a nationwide stirring began. The still-infant labor movement started to feel its muscle, in part because 1873 was another depression year, although Chicago—blessed with a unique position as a gathering and shipping center—was not quite so hard hit as the country's other major cities. Chicago still had lumber and cattle and grain to transport, and there was no complete paralysis of industry and trade.

By 1877, however, there were strikes on the railroads and trouble was brewing at the new McCormick Reaper works, now on Blue Island Avenue.

Opposite Page
Up, up, and away: The giant Ferris wheel, named for its Pittsburgh builder, was the single most popular attraction at the Columbian Exposition—with the possible exception of Little Egypt, the belly dancer.

James H. McVicker: The noted comedian and theater manager, and his freshly rebuilt theater.

The People's party voted Medill out of office in November and replaced him with a man of less puritanical ideals. Northwestern's School of Journalism was later named after him.

The Winds of Change: As early as March 30, 1873, the *Chicago Tribune* felt that the spirit of the city was different.

It is a common remark that Chicago was set forward ten years by the fire. The mingled town and village aspects are gone, with the buildings of the early days that held the latter character in the center of the city. The tendency is to the metropolitan in everything, buildings and their uses, stores and their occupants. And village notions are passing away with them. Even advertisers cease to insist on locations at easy distance from the Post Office, and a mile of our present area seems less than four or five blocks a few seasons ago. No one expects to know . . . half the audience at the church or theater, and as for knowing one's neighbors, that has become a lost art.

Oddly, Mayor Medill failed to realize that many Chicagoans, after working six days a week, needed relaxation on the seventh. Medill closed the saloons on Sunday in 1873, and Exposition Hall, which offered amusement as well as a number of educational and industrial displays, was also closed on the Sabbath. As a result of this action and his association with the newly formed Law and Order League (a sort of upper-echelon watchdog organization whose purpose was to suppress anything that distressed its founders), Medill became a one-term mayor.

Writing of the period in the lively *Chicago, The History of Its Reputation* with Henry Justin Smith, Lloyd Lewis says: "Wealth, the Protestant churches, and the Yankee aristocracy backed the Sunday closing, a situation which prompted spokesmen for the masses to declare: 'We are not against the arrest of Sunday drunks, but we are against the dictation of men who go to church on Sundays with long faces and then go to the Board of Trade on Monday to swindle their colleagues out of many bushels of grain.' "

A.C. Hesing, publisher of a German-language newspaper, aroused the Irish, Germans, and whatever liberals were called a century ago with a blistering attack on the Law and Order League. Hesing complained of the lack of inexpensive concerts and lectures for the working class and the efforts of the league to close the Exposition building on Sundays while failing to provide music in Lincoln Park for weekend strollers. He criticized laws closing the beer parlors on Sunday and concluded, "You are a pack of slaves if you suffer laws that prohibit this."

The police made an incredible 25,000 arrests during 1874, mostly for minor offenses. The majority of those picked up were unemployed. Lumberyard workers now made only 75 cents or $1 for a full day's work, and announcement that a new wage cut was imminent sent them out on strike. They returned almost immediately because of the scramble for their jobs.

Trouble Follows the Rails: The rail strikes in 1877 began in the East and soon spread west. There was a fight between police and striking railroad firemen in Baltimore in mid-July. A short while later Pittsburgh called out the militia to deal with strikers, and a reported $10-million worth of railroad property and equipment was destroyed. The *Chicago Daily News*, founded in 1876 and destined to become one of the world's best papers before it died a hundred years later, printed more accounts of the railroad troubles than any other paper in town—and sold for only one penny! As a result its circulation soared from 20,000 to more than 100,000 in short order.

So popular, in fact, was the *Chicago Daily News* with Chicago's working man that a group of businessmen waited on the editor, Melville E. Stone, with a strong request that the paper cease publication until the unrest was over. Stone's reply was as firm as that of Victor F. Lawson, the paper's owner. Both said no.

The committee's timing—if nothing else—was correct. They met with Stone and Lawson on July 23. That night there were mass meetings as a prelude to the walkout the next day of Michigan Central switchmen, told that their minuscule wages ($55 to $65 a month) were to be cut still lower.

Among the labor leaders (or agitators and anarchists as the business hierarchy called them) was Albert R. Parsons, a transplanted Texan and Confederate army veteran. A typesetter for the *Chicago Times* and unsuccessful candidate for alderman, he was a prominent member of the Workingman's party. Parsons was called in for an audience with Mayor Monroe Heath after the switchmen went on strike and told that he would be wise to go back to Texas at once "because those Board of Trade men would as leave hang you to a lamppost as not." Parsons said he'd stick around.

Despite apparent efforts by Parsons and other leaders to prevent violence, there was a clash between strikers and police at the McCormick plant on July 25. Chicago suddenly became a war zone. Twenty thousand police and armed volunteers carried arms as mobs of angry workers clashed with the militia and antistrike groups. The saloons were ordered closed. Citizens brought wagons and guns to police stations for use as needed, while Field and Leiter offered their dray horses and wagons as police conveyances. There were pitched battles on the Randolph Street bridge and at the viaduct near Archer and Halsted streets; locomotives were wrecked and shots fired at the Chicago, Burlington and Quincy roundhouse on West 16th Street.

The city's businessmen began demanding thousands of additional militiamen to combat "the ragged commune wretches." But Congressman Carter Harrison urged that police alone be used to quell the mob. Harrison said that the strike was started by laboring men, but was being aggravated by "idlers, thieves, and ruffians."

On Thursday, July 26, two companies of regular army troops came to town, and the strike collapsed. Perhaps 35 persons were killed during the trouble—none of them policemen. About 300 were arrested and later freed. Chicago was quiet again.

"Our Carter": Mayor Carter H. Harrison, Sr., who was said to have run a happy ship if not a particularly tidy one.

In 1879 the city's finances were so strained that many obligations were met in scrip. A newspaper commented: "The 'school marms' of Chicago have at last been paid a portion of their hard-earned and long-expected wages. There are still two months due these patient doves in the nursery of humanity."

In a gracious speech, Sherman said, "I believe Chicago would undertake to build a railroad to the moon, if the man in the moon would hold down a ladder long enough for the Mayor to get there."

Enter "Our Carter": Carter Henry Harrison, a worldly and urbane figure, was elected mayor in 1879, ending a parade of some 20 years of Republican mayors. In November of that year Harrison played host to a colorful and unusual affair, a Union Army reunion in the Palmer House. The event drew not only such nonmilitary figures as Mark Twain and the well-known atheist Robert Ingersoll, but also a glittering group of generals, among them U. S. Grant, William Sherman, Philip Sheridan, and John Logan.

Harrison was mayor for four consecutive terms and a fifth one later. His style—friendly, polished, and humorous—appealed to his constituents, as indeed did his personal honesty and the blandly permissive view he took of gambling, drinking, and houses of ill repute. Harrison and the town's foremost gambling boss, Mike McDonald (who ran a lucrative gaming parlor known with elegant simplicity as "the Store"), were often mentioned in the same breath, and there was no doubt that McDonald was a Harrison supporter. Yet the mayor never was accused of being "on the take"—a tradition that had not yet gained a noticeable foothold in the city.

By now Chicago had many fine hotels once more. These included the third Palmer House, its barber shop floor studded with genuine silver dollars; the Grand Pacific, said to be the first in town with flowers on the dining-room tables; the Sherman House, Briggs House, and (again) the fire-plagued Tremont. Many admired the Palmer House, on which Potter Palmer had lavished incredible sums, but others took a different view—particularly Rudyard Kipling, who obviously wouldn't have let Gunga Din spend a night in the place. In his *From Sea to Sea: Letters of Travel* (1899), Kipling called the hotel "a gilded and mirrored rabbit-warren." The acerbic Englishman also failed to find Chicago itself acceptable. "This place is the first American city I have encountered. . . . Having seen it, I urgently desire never to see it again."

Chicago reached the half-million mark in population (503,298) in 1890. Factories and business places became correspondingly larger, employing

many more workers. The old personal boss-worker relationship was passing from the scene, and the potential for labor trouble growing. The town had electric lights by the eighties, and about 5,000 telephones prior to 1886, but sanitation was so bad that half the city's children died before they were five years old. Deaths among young tenement dwellers outnumbered those in better residential areas by about three to one. Chicago was a real city now. It had slums.

Gone with the wind: Cyrus H. McCormick, inventor of the first really effective reaper, built this mammoth plant in time to free farm boys for the Union cause. This building burned in the Great Fire.

The Haymarket Bomb: The anarchist movement, which seemed to be losing much of its impetus for a time, was revived between 1884 and 1886 when business conditions again became depressed. Demands for an eight-hour day were insistent, and some firms complied. But in 1885, after Cyrus H. McCormick, Jr. succeeded his late father as president, the harvester plant refused to discharge five nonunion workers disliked by other employees because they supposedly were too friendly with a detested foreman. Workers

The detective Allan Pinkerton, a dedicated abolitionist, said, "John Brown is a greater man than Napoleon, and just as great as George Washington."

again went out (although their wages had recently been increased), and police, augmented by Pinkertons, came to guard the plant. This was particularly enraging to the estranged workers, for whom Pinkertons had become a spitting word because of their frequent use as strikebreakers.

The difficulty at the McCormick plant (which led to its closing by the management from February 16 to March 1) still continued on May 3, 1886, when the Lumber Shovers Union held an unrelated meeting about half a mile from the main gates. August Spies, a dedicated radical friendly with the lumberyard workers, was addressing them when the noon whistle blew at McCormick and nonstriking workers began to leave. They were rushed by some of the pickets, and fell back. Some of the mass-meeting crowd began to move toward the hubbub, but Spies told them that whatever was happening did not concern them. Then a policeman was shot, more police reinforcements began arriving, and a general fight broke out. Disregarding his own advice, Spies rushed over to watch and discovered that six of the strikers had been shot and killed. (There is dispute over this figure.) That evening circulars printed at Spies's anarchist *Arbeiter-Zeitung* proclaimed: "REVENGE! Working Men to Arms!!!" After an attack on the police and the "bosses," the appeal, written in both English and German, ended: "To arms we call you, to arms." Spies later said that the "REVENGE!" heading was added by one of the compositors without his knowledge.

The following day a second circular called for a turnout that evening at the Haymarket, as the block on Randolph Street between Desplaines and Halsted was known. This circular concluded: "Workingmen Arm Yourselves and Appear in Full Force!" Some copies had already been handed out before Spies (who had not written it) halted distribution long enough to take out the inflammatory sentence.

About 1,500 workingmen and their sympathizers, including some women, appeared for the rally. Spies was the first to hold forth, followed by Parsons; the crowd, however, remained unaroused. Then Samuel Fielden, a Methodist lay preacher who had been a weaver in England, began a fiery talk in which he suggested that "the law must be throttled, killed, and stabbed." This sent one of Police Inspector John Bonfield's undercover men hurrying to the Desplaines Street station, and Bonfield and 176 of his reinforcements moved out. It had now begun to rain, and the crowd began to break up.

As the police marched up Desplaines from Randolph, Capt. William Ward ordered the crowd to "disperse peacefully." Fielden had just shouted back that they *were* peaceful when some still unknown person lobbed a bomb into the ranks of the police. Shots were then fired from both sides. Fifteen minutes later, when the miniature battle ended, Officer Mathias Degnan was dead and

Prelude to tragedy: This provocative handbill, in German and English, summoned working men to the Haymarket.

A Short History of Chicago

60 other policemen and 12 civilians were injured.

Indicted for murder and conspiracy to murder were Spies, Parsons, Fielden, Michael Schwartz, an employee of the *Arbeiter-Zeitung*, toymaker George Engel, Adolph Fischer, a typesetter, Oscar Neebe, a well-to-do seller of yeast, and Louis Lingg and William Seliger, both carpenters. The last of the accused, Rudolph Schnaubelt, had fled to Europe by the time he was indicted.

Because Seliger turned state's evidence to avoid prosecution, only eight men went on trial in the courtroom of Judge Joseph E. Gary on July 15. Lingg roomed at Seliger's house and the two, according to Seliger's testimony, made bombs together. Although there was no credible evidence that any of the defendants threw the bomb or even conspired to do so, the jury brought in a verdict of guilty on August 19—after deliberating only three hours.

With equal speed, Judge Gary handed down sentences the next day, ordering Neebe to prison for 15 years and the other seven to the gallows. The execution date was set for November 11, but Gov. Richard Oglesby commuted the sentences of Schwartz and Fielden to life imprisonment the day before. Lingg, in whose cell police had earlier discovered four bombs, avoided the gallows by exploding a dynamite cap with his teeth. The hangings took place on schedule.

All efforts to prevent the death sentences from being carried out had failed, although a highly respectable committee helped finance a futile appeal to both state and federal supreme courts. Among those asking clemency were four circuit court judges, Potter Palmer and other prominent businessmen, and 16,000 Englishmen who signed petitions overseas.

The general opinion is that Lingg probably made the bomb for Schnaubelt. Parsons, incidentally, slipped away to Wisconsin after being arrested but joined his friends the day the hearing began.

In June 1893 Gov. John Altgeld issued pardons to the three anarchists still in prison—Neebe, Fielden, and Schwartz. With this act of conscience, Altgeld ruined his political career.

Birth of the Skyscraper: The turmoil over the Haymarket affair finally died down, and business went on as usual. But Chicago was now expanding upward as well as sideways. By the mid-eighties there were a number of changes in the city's skyline. George Pullman decided to erect a nine-story building at Adams and Michigan avenues as headquarters for his Pullman Palace Car Company. The structure offered not only a top-floor restaurant but large apartments as well. The Home Insurance Building—considered the prototype of the modern skyscraper—was completed in 1885. Designed by William Le Baron Jenney, it towered ten floors above the northeast corner of Adams and LaSalle. Jenney utilized the first steel beams ever made especially for the purpose; his design consisted basically of a steel skeleton with lightweight masonry as the sheath or outer skin. Another early architectural gem was the Rookery, opened in 1886. Its eleven floors accommodated 600 offices on the southeast corner of the same intersection. This work of

Phoenix—Chicago Style!

Delicate iron: Louis Sullivan, the genius who created this beautiful tracery for the Carson, Pirie, Scott building, died a penniless alcoholic.

Daniel W. Burnham and John H. Root was supported on a floating platform consisting of wood, iron, and concrete.

The young and brilliant Louis Sullivan was among the enterprising architects who flocked to Chicago in the wake of the Great Fire. He is most famous, perhaps, for the Auditorium Theater building at Michigan Avenue and Congress Street. Sullivan designed this combination opera house, hotel, and office building with his partner, Dankmar Adler, and it was dedicated in 1889. The year before, when the still-unfinished building was the site for the Republican National Convention, a reporter covering the event noted that "the faintest tremolo" of the band could be heard without trouble even in the galleries of the opera house.

The Auditorium posed difficult construction problems because of its immense bulk. Adler and Sullivan devised a floating platform about five feet thick of iron, wood, and concrete to compensate for the uncertain footing found when building so close to the lake. Adler also piled sufficient heavy material on top of the structure to equal the weight of the projected tower, which was added when the test load proved acceptable. Sullivan's mosaic decorations, one of the glories of the Auditorium, were composed of 15 million pieces of colored marble.

The wonders created for Chicago during this period by architects of the "Chicago School," as it came to be known, soon included the world's tallest building, Root's 20-story Masonic Temple at State and Randolph. The temple had 14 elevators capable of making the bottom-to-top round trip in three minutes and boasted hanging gardens on the roof.

The University of Chicago, a Baptist school that had suffered an untimely demise in 1886, came back to life in 1889 with the conditional donation of $600,000 by John D. Rockefeller, the brother-can-you-use-a-dime man. Rockefeller promised the money if the Baptists could raise another $400,000— which they did. Marshall Field also donated ten acres of land. In the same year, the Newberry Library, destined to become one of the world's finest research centers, had its start when 20 years of legal action failed to break the will of real estate pioneer Walter L. Newberry. The library named after him now stands where the home of Mahlon Ogden had been, one of the two North Side dwellings that survived direct attacks by the fire.

Not all the town's improvements involved steel and stone. In 1889 Jane Addams and Ellen Gates Starr, aided by other caring women, opened Hull House on South Halsted Street as a community service project working for political reform, improved garbage pickup, the end of sweatshops, the protection of children, and other desirable ends. The neighborhood, thronging with foreign-born Chicagoans, was mystified but grateful. It accepted Hull House cautiously, but eventually the settlement became a focal point for care of the sick, shelter for the homeless and abused, sewing and English language classes, book study programs, drama groups, and other gentle schemes to better the lives of those forced to live in such unlovely surroundings.

World's Columbian Exposition: The four hundredth anniversary of the discovery of the New World by Christopher Columbus was approaching, and Chicagoans were eager to have Congress name their city host for the proposed 1892 fair honoring the event. The city was

Sullivan arrived in 1873 and became a pupil of Jenney's before leaving for Paris and further study. He returned to Chicago in 1880.

About 2,000 persons in the city of one million had been dying of typhoid each year. By the end of the century, the Sanitary District had managed to reverse the flow of the Chicago River *away* from Lake Michigan—to contaminate the Mississippi instead of the city's drinking water.

"The finer and freer aspects of living must be incorporated into our common life and have free mobility through all elements of society if we would have our democracy endure."–Jane Addams

BIRD'S EYE VIEW OF THE WORLD'S COLUMBIAN EXPOSITION,

A Short History of Chicago

selected on the eighth ballot in 1890, defeating second-place New York 157 to 107. The site chosen was 600 acres of Jackson Park on the lakeshore, seven miles southeast of City Hall.

Preparations went ahead speedily with the precision of a well-planned military operation. Daniel W. Burnham of Root and Burnham was responsible for the final appearance of the fairgrounds from landscaping to buildings, while the major structures were designed by ten of the nation's leading architects and sculptors.

Women too were given an unexpectedly important role in planning the exposition. Mrs. Potter Palmer headed the Board of Lady Managers, a group consisting of about 175 women from 44 states and 3 territories. The architect for the Woman's Building, 22-year-old Sophia Hayden of Boston, was chosen after a number of female architects had submitted sketches.

Nineteen foreign countries and many of the states erected their own buildings, and 72 nations sent exhibits. Dedication of the partially completed layout was held in October 1892, with a crowd of 150,000 jammed into the Manufactures and Liberal Arts Building, the largest of its kind ever constructed. Its 44 acres of floor space used more than 3 million feet of lumber and five carloads of nails.

The "White City," as the fair was called, opened on schedule on May 1, 1893. At noon sharp President Cleveland flipped a switch of gold. Machinery began humming, flags were broken out on all the main buildings, statues were unveiled, and the guns of naval ships in the lake boomed in salute.

It seemed impossible that anyone, from anywhere, could have come to the exposition and not found a number of things to be fascinated by or to enjoy. The giant Ferris wheel, invented by a Pittsburgh engineer, was 250 feet in diameter and could accommodate 2,160 persons at one time. From the top position, riders could see Illinois, Indiana, Wisconsin, and Michigan.

There were the "solid" exhibits, such as machinery, paintings, sculpture, livestock, grain, typewriters, and all manner of manufactured articles. But there also were two alligators from Florida; three Cape Colony Zulus, demonstrating how gold was mined at the famous Kimberly diamond diggings in South Africa; the Windsor Castle tapestries, on loan from Queen Victoria herself; a $100,000 cocoa exhibit, with drinks "served by Dutch maidens in picturesque native attire"; captive balloon ascensions up to 1,000 feet; Baker's submarine craft, run by a crew of two men, which could remain underwater for 18 hours; and a small replica of the Blue Grotto of Capri.

Bolivian Indians were on view, one of them 9 feet 10 inches tall and weighing 418 pounds; the "pioneer" locomotive, from the early days of the Galena and Chicago Union Railroad; a continuous New England clambake; 100

Opposite page
Overview: One of the great man-made wonders of the last century.

Guns and corn: One of the fair's biggest attractions was the 120-ton gun built by the Krupp factory in Germany, the world's biggest at 57 feet, breech to muzzle. Its missiles could penetrate 18 inches of steel. A comforting contrast was the Woman's Corn Kitchen, which illustrated "the many palatable forms the great staple of the country can be made to yield in the hands of a good cook."

manuscripts, autograph letters, rare books, and other documents dealing with Columbus; a Dahomey Village, with 80 New Guinea natives; Des Moines in miniature; and a 20-foot-high model of the Eiffel Tower.

There was an Irish lace exhibit; an Iowa Corn Palace; a huge map made of pickles, with lakes and rivers of vinegar; a 21-ton block of bituminous coal from the state of Washington; the genuine Liberty Bell, crack and all; and a loft of homing pigeons released from time to time and clocked in on their return. In the Woman's Building there were more than 200 paintings by female artists of the state; John Jacob Astor sent along some of his inventions, including a new bicycle brake and a contraption to dust macadam roads by means of blasts of air; and of course there were the sideshow attractions on the Midway, among them the Midget Village.

If you still had an appetite after seeing the National Prison Association exhibit of jail cells and a collection of punishment devices, "including a wonderful array of old-time instruments of torture," you could dine in the Great White Horse Inn, as described in Dickens's *Pickwick Papers*. There were plenty of eating places. The official souvenir guide book, complete with map of the grounds and a list of all the sights, declared that 60,000 hungry persons could be served at the same time.

The total cost of the World's Columbian Exposition, whose attendance of 27,529,400 came very close to matching that of the Paris Exposition of 1889, was $26 million. Not to worry. The stockholders saw all their money again, plus about 10 percent interest.

There were some very complimentary things said about how the fair was run and what there was to see. But no one topped the remark of one out-of-town customer to his wife as they were departing. "Well, Susan," he said, "it paid, even if it did take all the burial money."

Travel to, from, and in the exposition was possible by road, rail, gondola, a movable sidewalk, and a rolling chair.

There was a tragedy the night of October 28. Carter Harrison, who had addressed a meeting of fellow mayors at the fair, was killed by a disappointed and crazed office seeker.

"City on the Make"

Less than four years after the murder of his father, Carter H. Harrison, Jr., ran for mayor of Chicago. The younger Harrison, a lawyer and real-estate man, and his brother, William Preston Harrison, had first tried vainly to put the *Chicago Times* (purchased by their father in 1891 for an overpriced $265,000) on a sound financial footing. Just within sight of a break-even point, they were forced to sell in 1895 at a distress figure.

Advertising boycotts were a principal reason for the paper's lack of success. Many advertisers had been angered when the *Chicago Times* backed the workers during the Pullman strike of 1894. Like the labor unrest in Chicago in the seventies and eighties, this famous strike resulted from hard economic times. As sales of his Pullman Palace car slumped disastrously during the depression of 1894, George M. Pullman cut wages and fired employees. A bright but greedy man, he refused to deal with the strikers or do anything to alleviate the plight of those who found themselves penniless in his town of Pullman, which—as its founder admitted—was not run as a philanthropic venture. Those living there paid above-average rental for their cottages, and only a handful of families could afford the $3 annual fee for use of the library.

Despite a sympathy strike by members of Eugene V. Debs's American Railway Union (to which many of Pullman's men belonged), the walkout was broken. Over the protests of Governor Altgeld and Mayor John P. Hopkins, President Cleveland sent federal troops as strikebreakers on, ironically, the Fourth of July. Found guilty of violating an injunction forbidding interference with the trains, Debs served six months in the Woodstock, Illinois, jail. Pleas from across the nation had failed to make Pullman yield a centimeter or show the slightest compassion for the hungry families. Even the conservative industrialist Mark Hanna remarked during a speech to the Union League Club in

Opposite page
The boss: Al Capone, who was obeyed by cops, judges, politicians, and his own hoodlum army until the Feds nailed him—on an income tax rap.

Pullman: The town George Pullman built for his employees. Pullman perfected the sleeping car, but found no formula for making the workers love him.

Cleveland: "A man who won't meet his own men halfway is a goddamn fool!"

Three years later, in 1897, Carter Harrison actively supported Judge John B. Payne for mayor. But he and Payne had a falling out, and Harrison became a candidate for the office which he had intended to seek only at some future date. Although making his first bid for election, Harrison was as sure-footed as a veteran campaigner. When he discovered that his most-feared rival, former alderman John M. Harlan, appealed to younger voters because he had played guard on the Princeton football team, Harrison, an avid cyclist, posed astride a racing bike complete with cap, sweater, knickers, mustache, and a turtleneck sweater from which hung a pendant with 18 bars, each representing a "run" with the Century Road Club. The photograph then was lithographed and used as a campaign poster bearing the legend: "Not the Champion Cyclist, but the Cyclists' Champion."

Harrison's mayoral run was aided by two improbable eccentrics: John (Bathhouse John) Coughlin and Michael (Hinky-Dink) Kenna, the flamboyant and unscrupulous aldermen of the notorious 1st Ward. They later not only gave him valuable votes in the City Council but also kept him amused during his years in office.

It may have been the large German vote, however, which put him over. Harrison was fluent in that language since he had lived in Germany for months as a youth. He could sing German songs and drink German beer. Like his father before him, he was known for his easygoing attitude toward personal liberties which did not affect those of other people—such as selling beer on Sunday.

Responding to his promises of a possible eight-hour workday, better garbage collections, a relaxed administration, and aid for newly arrived immigrants, his supporters gave Harrison 5,000 more votes than the combined total of his three opponents. Harrison, the first Chicago-born mayor, took office in April 1897. The city's population was 1,490,937.

Labor leader: Eugene V. Debs, president of the American Railway Union, was sentenced to six months in jail in the aftermath of the Pullman strike of 1894.

Yerkes Is Derailed: The new mayor promptly began what turned out to be a long feud with Charles T. Yerkes, who had come to town from Philadelphia in 1881 and soon gained control of almost all the city's streetcar lines. Yerkes, a rich and plausible scoundrel with many connections in the business community, was not a Harrison backer. But he still had high hopes for the passage in Springfield of the Humphrey bill, which would have extended streetcar franchises throughout the state to 100 years—80 more than his present one called for—with no additional cost to Yerkes except what he was handing out under the table.

Chicago's hungriest aldermen—who were in the majority—didn't want the Humphrey bill passed. By taking the franchise out of their control, it would have *given* Yerkes something they much preferred to *sell* him. In consequence they offered no objection when Mayor Harrison named a small group of their honest colleagues to the committee which left with him for Springfield each Monday night after the Council meeting to lobby against the bill.

When its obvious illegality grew too apparent, the Humphrey bill finally was withdrawn and the Allen bill, giving Illinois municipalities the right to extend their rail franchises up to a total of 50 years, was introduced in its stead. This still pleased Yerkes and delighted the "gray wolves"(as the more sticky-fingered Chicago aldermen were known).

With impetus from Yerkes's slush fund, the state legislature happily made the Allen bill law. But some strenuous arm-twisting by Mayor Harrison brought some of the "wolves" to the other side of the fence. Following a municipal election in which Yerkes not only failed to unseat hostile councilmen but also lost some of his allies, it quickly became evident that there was no chance of the current franchise being extended. Even if the council had voted for such an extension, there was the certainty of a mayoral veto. And the jubilant Harrison, indicating his hat on the desk, told newsmen: "If Yerkes can pass an ordinance over my veto, I'll eat that brown fedora!"

Never one to ignore reality, Yerkes soon sold his street railway stock for a fortune and took off for England. He was hard at work helping to build the London Underground when he died in 1905 at the age of 75.

"Bet your bottom dollar you lose the blues . . .": This song from the flapper era remains the most famous (and merriest) ever written about Chicago.

"The habits of the genuine Chicagoan are characteristic. He dines at noon whether he is a banker or a laborer, and eats three hearty meals a day; but not to collide with eastern ways too directly, he calls his supper 'dinner,' and his dinner 'lunch.' [He] will forgive anything but undiluted affectation."—Moran's *Dictionary of Chicago* (1909)

Death in the Afternoon: Life had become more peaceful for Mayor Harrison, but in 1903 one of the greatest tragedies ever visited upon Chicago marred his fourth term. The new and luxurious Iroquois Theater on Randolph Street was offering an extravaganza called "Mr. Bluebeard," starring the popular Eddie Foy, during the Christmas holidays. The December 30th matinee drew a standing-room crowd consisting largely of mothers and children and school groups accompanied by teachers.

During the second act, while a chorus was singing "In the Pale Moonlight," there was a wisp of smoke on stage and a sudden flicker of flame. What later was described as the only gas jet in use (or a short in the electrical circuitry) had started a piece of scenery burning. Foy stepped to the footlights and called out, "Please be quiet! There is no danger!" And he told the orchestra to play on. But the fire spread rapidly to other sets, the lights went out and the asbestos curtain halted while only halfway down. Then the panic began.

As the audience fled, a torrent of flame and poisonous fumes poured from beneath the curtain into the auditorium and up to the gallery. Those desperately seeking exits found some locked and failed to find others, hidden by heavy draperies. There also were closed gates, intended to prevent galleryites from sneaking down in quest of better seats. When the flames in the "fireproof" theater were out—perhaps as soon as 15 minutes after the first alarm was sounded—602 of the estimated 1,200 patrons were dead, 180 of them heaped on the grand stairway leading to the main floor.

Harrison, out of town when the Iroquois burned, returned the following day and at once inspected the disaster scene. He reported little visible evidence of fire, other than in the front rows of the gallery and parquette. Seemingly, panic and fumes had killed most of the victims, in what still is the third worst theater fire recorded anywhere.

Attempts to hold Harrison, the theater owners, and fire department officials blameworthy quickly failed. The catastrophe did lead to improved theater safety around the world, with newly established regulations demanding flameproof scenery, automatic sprinklers, and steel curtains across the stage.

A Man of Integrity: Harrison remained mayor until 1905, when he decided not to run and was given a testimonial dinner by the largely Republican City Council. Pleasantly enough, the *Chicago Tribune*, a longtime Harrison critic, ran an editorial praising him. "He is as poor a man today as he was when he went into office, poor in everything, indeed, except in reputation. . . . He is now known as not merely a man of integrity, but one of ability and administrative capacity."

Six years later, however, when Harrison again sought the mayor's office and was opposed by Prof. Charles Merriam of the University of Chicago, the *Chicago Tribune* began a series of stories covering his four terms in office. Its author seemingly had neglected to read the *Chicago Tribune*'s editorial commenting on the mayor's honesty; he charged that during one race Harrison's campaign manager accepted a $500 contribution from a saloonkeeper whose license had been revoked—and that the license then was reinstated.

Since the license in question had *not* been restored, the charge obviously was false, and Harrison sued the paper for libel—$100,000 worth. The *Chicago Tribune* defiantly reprinted earlier hostile stories and cartoons involving the mayor that had run in the Hearst press. Harrison raised the amount he demanded to $200,000. The *Chicago Tribune* printed more second-hand accounts. Harrison boosted the ante to $300,000, and eventually the newspaper cancelled the series with an apology and a complete retraction. Harrison went on to his first four-year term, defeating Merriam, a thoroughly worthy opponent, by about 18,000 votes.

Harrison was less easygoing than he had been, at least when it came to the Levee, as the South Side vice district was known. In 1911, to the surprise of some and the dismay of others, he ordered the luxurious Everleigh Club on

Minna and Ada's place: The notorious Everleigh Club is at the far right, on the 2100 block of Dearborn.

Papa Bear: On July 24, 1915, the excursion steamer *Eastland* suddenly capsized at the dock, killing 812 people. Among the lucky that day was the late George Halas, founder of the Chicago Bears and one of professional football's pioneers. He arrived too late to board.

One irate tavern owner, George ("Cap") Streeter, defied all orders to close, saying his saloon was not in Chicago but in the District of Lake Michigan, which he had claimed years before when sands built up around his wrecked boat north of the river and east of Michigan Avenue.

Dearborn closed down. One of the country's most notorious bagnios, the Everleigh was opened in 1900 by Minna and Ada Everleigh, two Texas madames. Their undoing was a brochure, with full-page illustrations of the Turkish, Japanese, and Persian rooms and the Room of a Thousand Mirrors and—the final insult perhaps—the statement that the two outstanding attractions in town were the Union Stockyards and the Everleigh Club.

Before his term expired Harrison also closed a number of drinking places as well as the restaurant on South Wabash Avenue run by "Big Jim" Colosimo. Big Jim's was shut down for failure to obey the closing laws and for other previously overlooked violations.

Send in the Clowns: Seeking an unprecedented sixth term, Harrison was beaten in the 1915 primary by Robert M. Sweitzer, once a Cook County clerk. Sweitzer was then defeated in the general election by William ("Big Bill") Thompson.

Thompson's curious career offers many of the elements of a minor Greek tragedy. He had it all to start with—wealth, position, the admiration of his fellows. He had everything going for him but common sense. Big Bill could have been so much more, and he could have left Chicago a better city because he had been its leader. Instead, he turned into a buffoon.

"Unpredictable" might be the polite word for Thompson in the mayor's chair. Although his first announcement after victory was assurance that "crooks had better move out," Big Jim Colosimo's Wabash Avenue spot soon reopened. Thompson scored points by settling the 11,000-man streetcar strike in June 1915, then enraged the drinking classes by ordering all taverns closed on Sundays. Representing a group of the city's tavern owners, Anton J. Cermak produced a written agreement signed by Thompson only two weeks before the election in which he promised not to enforce Sunday closings. Big Bill replied that he couldn't remember signing any such pledge and that anyway he didn't wish to break state laws.

In an era of municipal improvement, Thompson was anathema to those who liked good government. Critics pointed to thousands of "temporary" employees he hired during his first five months in office. Civil service personnel were fired to make room for these patronage jobs.

In 1916 Thompson and his police chief were investigated by the state's attorney, whose raiders invaded City Hall to seize a variety of records, some purporting to show that South Side brothels were paying hefty sums each week for protection. Police Chief Healey was acquitted of graft charges, but Thompson had no difficulty finding more problems. After the United States

Mayor and flier: Mayor Thompson introducing Charles Lindbergh to a Comiskey Park throng a few months after Lindy's sensational trans-Atlantic flight in 1927.

declared war against Germany, he gave speeches opposing the draft and refused to invite important French officials to visit Chicago during their American tour though he later changed his mind.

In consequence, Mayor Thompson was expelled from membership in the Rotary Club; the Illinois Athletic Club removed his photograph from its walls; and the bishop of Baltimore (in a surprisingly un-Christian moment) suggested he be shot as a traitor. Then the Society of Veterans of Foreign Wars hanged him in effigy on the lakefront for allowing a pacifist rally to be held.

Under Big Bill's two laid-back, hail-fellow-well-met terms, prostitution, gambling, and bootlegging flourished. In 1923 he decided not to run again, largely because of rigged contracts and phony bids involving the schools by some of his associates. Although he would make a comeback in 1927 with the help of his friend Al Capone, Big Bill's career would be all downhill after this final victory.

World War I increased the demand for labor, and 50,000 blacks moved to Chicago, doubling the city's black population. Big Bill's second term was tarnished in 1919 by Chicago's first major race riot.

Hit Time in the Old Town: When Prohibition went into effect on February 16, 1920, the gangs, well established under Thompson, were ready to help ease the city's thirst. It is said sometimes that Prohibition created the gangsters of Chicago, but this is not quite true. Prohibition was simply the factor that brought them out of the wings onto center stage and made them rich and powerful.

By 1920 Chicago already had many hard characters, many of them imported during the newspaper circulation wars earlier in the century. The principal battles were between Hearst's *Chicago Examiner* strong-arm squads and those of the *Chicago Tribune,* with both sides intimidating truck drivers, newsdealers, and even newsboys. After the circulation battles ended, many of the hired troublemakers remained, among them a native Chicagoan, former choirboy Dion O'Banion.

Ambitious hoodlums also came to Chicago to work for men like Big Jim Colosimo, a devotee of opera and an entrepreneur in gambling joints and bawdy houses. Big Jim's popular eating place on South Wabash Avenue was patronized by dozens of prominent Chicagoans. His restaurant was safely within the confines of the notoriously permissive 1st Ward, run with gusto by aldermen Mike (Hinky-Dink) Kenna and Bathhouse John Coughlin.

Despite his possession of early Chicago clout, Big Jim became the target for some small-time Black Hand extortioners. After paying once or twice, he apparently lost patience. In 1909 he invited his nephew, a tough New Yorker named Johnny Torrio, to move to Chicago. A couple of the Black Hand collectors were soon ambushed and blown away, and Torrio began helping Colosimo with his multifarious enterprises.

But upon falling in love, the burly (and already married) Colosimo lost interest in his lucrative underworld activities. Torrio became vexed. In 1919 Johnny in turn sent to New York for help, importing one Al Brown—also known as Al Capone—a young torpedo already in trouble with the law there. Capone became a bodyguard and chauffeur for Torrio, who by this time was branching out for himself, although there was no apparent break with his uncle.

In 1920 Torrio told Big Jim that two truckloads of liquor would soon arrive at the restaurant. Colosimo was on hand to receive the shipment—as well as a fusillade of bullets from the customary unknown assailant. The mourners at Big Jim's funeral included three judges, an assistant state's attorney, and a number of aldermen.

Capone Takes Cicero: Big Bill Thompson was succeeded in 1923 by an honest man, Judge William E. Dever. The new mayor closed so many speakeasies that Torrio and Capone, who was rapidly moving up in the underworld ranks, grew unhappy. Torrio moved mob operations to Cicero, and in the spring of 1924, using squads of goons as persuaders, Capone so influenced the Cicero municipal election that only candidates favorable to a wide-open town achieved office. Capone must have felt at home in the suburb,

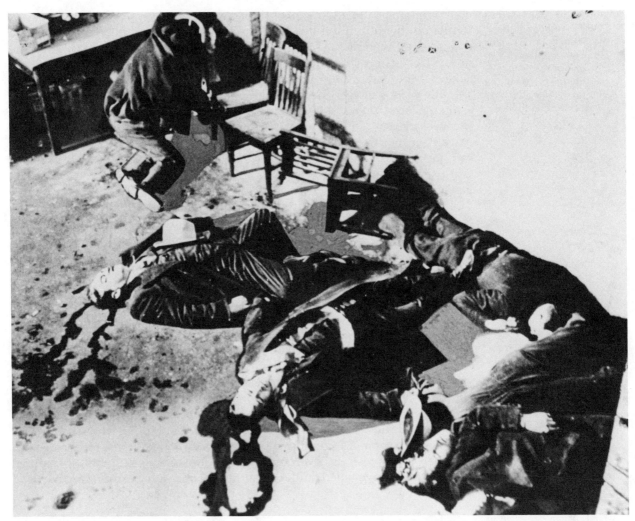

where he set up his headquarters in the reinforced Hawthorne Inn. Cicero now boasted more than 150 speakeasies.

The Chicago gangs argued frequently over territorial rights. Early in 1924 Johnny Torrio was caught by police while directing the loading of liquor trucks. His enemy O'Banion was also arrested, but Torrio later learned that Dion had tipped off the raiders.

The situation finally exploded on November 10, 1924. O'Banion was in his North Side flower shop opposite Holy Name Cathedral, where he spent his

Massacre on St. Valentine's: Five members of the George "Bugs" Malone mob, plus an innocent bystander, were cut down by executioners masquerading as policemen. Capone was suspected of having orchestrated the affair.

more reputable moments. Two or three men entered (possibly some of the six Genna brothers from the West Side, with whom he had been feuding). The men seemed friendly, so O'Banion accepted an outstretched hand. Then the fireworks began. O'Banion's ostentatious funeral, attended by friend and foe alike, set the pattern for many more to come.

The next year three of the Gennas died from what then could be considered natural causes. After a close call with rival gunmen, Torrio too decided to retire from the Chicago wars, leaving the 26-year-old Capone top man. On November 20, 1926, Hymie Weiss boldly invaded Cicero with a convoy of autos carrying troops. This expeditionary force riddled the Hawthorne Inn, but Capone was safely dining in a nearby restaurant. Weiss himself was dispatched near Holy Name Cathedral a few weeks later.

The sound of gunfire continued unabated into the early thirties, with one four-year stretch recording 200 killings—without a single conviction. Two were particularly flamboyant. In the 1929 St. Valentine's Day massacre, seven men were machine-gunned in a North Side warehouse during trouble between George "Bugs" Moran and Capone, and in June 1930 Alfred "Jake" Lingle, a *Chicago Tribune* reporter, was gunned down at noon in the underground approach to the Illinois Central suburban station near the public library.

Most of the St. Valentine's Day victims were members of Moran's gang, waiting to unload an expected shipment of bootleg liquor. The executioners all were dressed as policemen. Upon hearing the news, Moran's reaction was a laconic "Only Capone kills like that."

At first it was believed that Lingle, a well-known man-about-town and the *Chicago Tribune*'s authority on police and gangsters, was killed because of his newspaper connections. The *Chicago Tribune* immediately offered a $25,000 reward. Unfortunately, the paper soon learned that Lingle (whose salary was $65 weekly) had bank accounts in the thousands and played the races constantly. When it was also discovered that he had been a close friend of Capone, much of the outrage faded, as did the aura of martyrdom surrounding the dead newsman.

A First: A happier event in 1928 was the election of the first black congressman from above the Mason-Dixon line: Oscar DePriest of Chicago. He was the first black to serve in Congress since George Henry White, elected during Reconstruction.

Have Gun, Must Travel: The Depression spawned a new type of gangster—the bank robber. The best known of these was John Dillinger, a farm boy from Indiana who had gone to prison for a bungled bank holdup and formed his gang from fellow ex-convicts. Despite an unrelenting FBI quest, Dillinger and his band of pillagers roved the Midwest during the 1930s. Anointed "Public Enemy No. 1," Dillinger broke out of jail in Crown Point, Indiana, with a wooden gun and nonwooden money and later shot his way out of a federal trap at Little Bohemia near Mercer, Wisconsin. He was finally betrayed in 1934 at Chicago's Biograph Theater by Anna Sage, the notorious "Lady in Red," who had traded information to the G-Men to avoid deportation.

Dillinger was a child of the Depression and, in a way, a symbol of the era. Many viewed him as a kind of Robin Hood and saw his exploits as a sort of rough justice: he was robbing the banks that had robbed them in the closings that followed the crash of '29.

The Dismal Decade: The paper profits so many Americans had amassed in frenetic Wall Street trading blew away on that black October Friday in 1929 when the market suffered its worst mauling in history. Harold M. Mayer and Richard G. Wade summarize the impact on Chicago admirably in their *Growth of a Metropolis.*

> The immediate jolt was severe. But worse still, recovery was nowhere in sight. Every year after 1929 seemed a step down. By 1933, employment in the city's industry had been cut in half; payrolls were down almost seventy-five percent. Foreclosures jumped from 3,148 in 1929 to 15,200 four years later; over 163 banks, most located in the outlying areas, closed their doors.

Many failed to pay rent or mortgages and were dispossessed. This misfortune was so widespread that the Chicago Urban League found "every available dry spot and every bench on the west side of Washington Park covered by sleepers." Newspaper photographs from the early 1930s show the spreading multitude of the homeless. Bedclothes for many are old newspapers and tattered rags. In one poignant shot, dead-eyed men watch as police burn the cardboard shelters they had erected in a city park.

In his meticulously detailed history of the *Chicago Tribune,* Lloyd Wendt describes how the "unemployed scoured the streets and alleys for firewood and scraps of garbage, and thousands of jobless men slept under double-decked Wacker Drive and Michigan Avenue, which became known as the 'Hoover Hotel.'" A grim joke summed up the almost universal despair. A man is about to register for a hotel room, but the clerk needs further information: "For sleeping or jumping, sir?"

Even the very rich were affected. Col. Robert McCormick, publisher of the *Chicago Tribune,* sold the unprofitable *Liberty* magazine, abolished the paper's annual bonus, and cut staff salaries. Samuel Insull, the utilities millionaire who fled to Europe when his empire collapsed, was only one of the formerly

Anna (who was no lady and didn't wear red) was eventually deported anyway. Once each year, on the anniversary of Dillinger's death, the Biograph shows *Manhattan Melodrama,* the film playing that day—at the 1934 price of 25 cents. The folk hero's original tombstone, chipped away by souvenir hunters, is in Joseph Pinkston's Dillinger Museum at Nashville, Indiana.

Insull was extradited but cleared of any wrongdoing. He died in Paris with less than 27 cents in his pocket.

wealthy wiped out by the depression.

Franklin Roosevelt was elected president in 1932 and promptly began a series of programs that brought hope to the nation. These actions, while furiously attacked by those who didn't need them, helped until World War II brought economic relief.

RRMcC: Some patriots were outraged that *Chicago Tribune* owner Col. Robert McCormick permitted the Japanese government to rent office space in the Tribune Tower. They did not know that the U.S. government received valuable information from the bugged rooms.

The new paper held its own and, as the *Chicago Sun-Times,* was still vital in 1983 when the Field brothers sold it to press lord Rupert Murdoch.

Chicago Enters the War: The prospect of entry into the European war—even against such an obvious menace as Nazi Germany—filled many Chicagoans with dismay. The America First Committee, headed by Sears, Roebuck president Gen. Robert E. Wood, campaigned for isolationism. The *Chicago Tribune* ran antiwar editorials, pointing out that the nation was ill-equipped for the struggle. Indeed, the paper's statewide poll early in the European conflict showed that 74 percent of those questioned believed America should remain uninvolved. Dubious about the *Chicago Tribune*'s findings, Robert Maynard Hutchins of the University of Chicago commissioned a poll of his own. This showed 74.7 percent opposed to American participation in the war. Interventionists detested the *Chicago Tribune* and welcomed the appearance in 1941 of Marshall Field's prowar *Chicago Sun.*

After the Japanese attack on Pearl Harbor, however, Chicagoans gave whole-hearted support to the war effort. Among American cities, Chicago set a record by spending $1.3 billion for war plants; its workers turned out airplane engines and other material in huge quantities. The mammoth Stevens Hotel was requisitioned to train servicemen, while the Chicago Beach Hotel became a military hospital and the Auditorium Theater a recreation center, its stage converted into bowling alleys. Two old passenger ships were refurbished as training vessels for future aircraft carrier crews, and war bond rallies raised huge sums from enthusiastic citizens. The *Chicago Tribune*, which did an about-face after Pearl Harbor, sometimes supplied war correspondents as speakers.

The city's most definitive wartime contribution came from a secret laboratory under the stands at Stagg Field at the University of Chicago. There, on December 2, 1942, the atomic age was born when a group of scientists led by Enrico Fermi split the atom.

The war brought prosperity to the city and helped begin the breakdown of racial barriers. Black and white soldiers trained in the same camps and fought on the same fronts. Chicago blacks who returned from overseas were no longer fearful targets for racial slurs, although they returned to segregation in many areas, including the almost completely black South Side. There was trouble in Bridgeport, Trumbull Park, and West Side neighborhoods when blacks seek-

A Short History of Chicago

ing to escape from Chicago ghettoes attempted to move in.

Threats of boycotts of white businesses caused some Chicago offices to reluctantly sprinkle in a few black employees. But for Chicago the war was at least a real beginning toward the destruction of the city's notoriously rigid segregation patterns.

ANew Era Begins: When Thompson died in 1944, a *Chicago Daily News* editorial called him "the most unbelievable man in Chicago history." The *Chicago Sun-Times* report that only 32 mourners had shown up on the second night of the wake rekindled memories of better days. Carter Harrison, Jr., and Gov. Dwight Green came to the funeral, and in his eulogy the minister declared: "Thompson is just another word for Americanism as he saw it."

Mayor Edward Kelly, who served from 1933 to 1947, has been compared to a watered-down Big Bill Thompson. By the time Kelly was nearing the end of his last term, he had fallen out of favor with the electorate, largely because of his outspoken stand for public housing in a community that has never regarded the idea with much enthusiasm. Under pressure, Kelly decided not to run again; the Democrats slated Martin H. Kennelly, a respected but colorless businessman. Kennelly served two lackluster terms before he was succeeded by Richard J. Daley, the 51-year-old chairman of the Cook County Democratic Central Committee and a consummate politician.

Daley was to become Chicago's longest-serving, most controversial mayor, and he moved into office with the assurance of a monarch ascending to the throne. He was serving his sixth term—a Chicago record—when he had a fatal heart attack in his physician's office on December 20, 1976.

Anton Cermak succeeded Big Bill in 1931. In February 1933, while next to President-elect Franklin D. Roosevelt in an open touring car, he was shot by an assassin who was aiming at FDR. Cermak died in March; Kelly served the remainder of his term, then was elected three times in his own right.

GOOD FOR CHICAGO

Re-Elect   **MAYOR**
RICHARD J.

DALEY

DEMOCRATIC PRIMARY
TUESDAY, FEBRUARY 25th

A Long Reign, a Hard Snow, and Two Chicago Firsts

9

Following his election in 1955 Daley quickly became the undisputed boss of "The City That Works." While obviously more concerned with cement and steel than with the plight of those living in substandard homes in the ghetto, Daley managed to enlist the support of big business, bankers, and labor chieftains. On the surface, at least, Chicago moved along with a serenity envied by most of the nation's other large cities.

Daley's first five years went smoothly enough despite a surprisingly tough showing by Republican Robert Merriam in the 1960 mayoral election. In that year, however, one of Daley's greatest political weapons—refusal to deal with any facts he didn't want to meet—backfired. He had scoffed at Merriam's claims of police corruption and praised the Chicago force as one of the country's finest. But then a small-time thief, Richard Morrison, was arrested and began talking so frantically that he quickly became known as "the Babbling Burglar." Morrison implicated eight policemen from the Summerdale Station as his eager accomplices, alleging that they not only gave him orders for particular items they wanted stolen, but even used squad cars to carry the loot.

These disclosures, and their continuing ramifications in the newspapers, upset Mayor Daley. After the first shock he appointed the customary blue ribbon committee to recommend a new police chief. Chairman of the committee was Prof. Orlando W. Wilson, head of the criminology department at the University of California. When the deliberations ended, his fellow members urged that Wilson himself be given the job.

This could hardly have surprised Daley (he had asked Wilson to head the committee), but it probably surprised the department, which the new superintendent promptly shook so hard that its collective teeth rattled. There were transfers, new appointments, and a number of retirements, and memories of

Probably the world's busiest airport, O'Hare International opened in 1955. It was named for Congressional Medal of Honor winner Edward (Butch) O'Hare, a navy pilot killed at the Battle of Midway. For some unknown reason, Mayor Daley always referred to the airport as "O'Hara."

Opposite page
Familiar face: Richard J. Daley, one of the most famous mayors in American history. He was elected six times and served 21 years.

the Babbling Burglar and his revelations gradually faded as the department improved. Daley had surmounted his most formidable hurdle to that point in the manner usual to the owners of losing ball teams—he simply replaced the coach.

Jetstream Jesse: Civil rights leader, founder of Chicago's Operation PUSH, and a candidate for the presidency, Jackson cut his political teeth on sixties strife.

The Protests Erupt: By the 1960s Chicago's black citizens were beginning to take the civil rights movement very seriously. They were discovering their latent power at the polls and were understandably discontented with being at the end of every line in town. In 1964 there was even an attempt to integrate Bridgeport, Mayor Daley's home turf. A white activist bought a small apartment building a block or so from the Daley residence and quietly rented to two young black students. There were ugly demonstrations for a couple of days, and then the police "solved" the problem. The blacks returned home a few days after moving in and found that the cops had moved them out and that their apartment had been rented to a white tenant.

The next attempt to educate the area came in 1965, when Dick Gregory, the noted comedian, led a parade through Bridgeport. When it was met with violence, there were arrests—but only of the marchers. Although the demonstrations continued, the violence suddenly vanished, presumably at the order of someone living in the area. Daley blamed the protests on Communists backed by Republican money.

It was one of those long, hot summers, and Chicago blacks joined in the riots sweeping the country's major cities. There was a very clear message in the burning and looting, but Daley didn't seem to get it. His intimates admitted privately that he was angry with Superintendent Wilson for not ordering tougher police tactics.

Daley said the trouble was simply "a question of lawlessness, hoodlumism, and hooliganism."

In 1966 Dr. Martin Luther King, Jr., came to Chicago to promote integration. While outwardly polite, Daley was furious, and off the record he referred to King in highly uncomplimentary terms. The situation grew more intense during the summer, culminating in widespread looting, arson, and random sniping before the National Guard ended the outbreak.

Typically, after declaring that "outsiders" were largely responsible for the trouble, Daley met with Dr. King and assured King he was not to blame. The result of the meeting was a citywide turn-on-the-hydrants program and the installation of portable swimming pools in the poorer neighborhoods. But the marches and the violence—much of it caused by whites attacking black protesters—went on. Eventually conferences, double-talk, and the coming of cooler weather, plus Dr. King's departure, brought an uneasy and temporary peace.

After Wilson resigned in 1967, the police reverted to their pre-Wilson attitudes toward demonstrations. They undoubtedly were encouraged in this by Daley's public statement about Dr. King: "We don't need him to tell us what to do. . . . he only comes here . . . to cause trouble."

King was assassinated in Memphis on April 4, 1968, and the next day brought wild riots in cities from coast to coast. Daley and Fire Commissioner Robert Quinn, his longtime chum, flew low over the blazing and tumultuous blocks of the West Side, where Daley saw residents fleeing with stolen property. Quinn told him that firemen were being shot at while trying to put out the flames. When the flight ended Daley announced that arsonists were to be shot and killed on sight and looters shot but not killed. The outcry against this order was citywide and colored both black and white. The mayor backed down when the controversy grew and the rioting slackened, saying he had been "misunderstood." Once again there was an uneasy peace.

Daley's press chief, Earl Bush, said the press was at fault for not realizing the intent of Daley's order. "It was damn bad reporting," he charged. "They should have printed what he meant, not what he said."

Violence in Blue: But the year was not yet over. Less than three weeks after Dr. King's death, the police ferociously attacked marchers in a Chicago Peace Council rally protesting the Vietnam War. No official action was taken against this surprising onslaught, and reports of witnesses and victims were largely discounted because it all seemed so improbable. The police assault set the precedent for the sorry spectacle which took place during the Democratic National Convention late in August. By the time the convention opened, the city was crowded with antiwar activists, some smart and some stupid, and the city's 12,000 policemen, some smart and some stupid, were put on 12-hour shifts. In addition there were National Guardsmen and regular army troops by the thousands available, and when Daley refused to consider negotiation meetings with the 5,000 or so out-of-town protesters, trouble was virtually guaranteed.

The police were well armed and organized. The protesters were poorly organized and were satisfied, for the most part, to fight with words, a refusal to obey police orders, and the hurling of rocks and filth. The hippies, to use that now outmoded word, established Lincoln Park as their gathering place. Citing the usually overlooked 11 P.M. vacate-the-park rule, the police swept through and clubbed and routed them on Sunday night, the day the convention opened. Newsmen and photographers were prime targets for the free-swinging cops. There was more fighting that Tuesday night, and Wednesday evening the whole affair moved onto the nation's television screens as police attacked regardless of race, sex, or common sense, using clubs, mace, fists, and feet. Press credentials were an invitation to be clubbed, and fleeing meant, in many cases, simply adding the joy of the chase.

Chicago Seven plus One: The defendants and their attorney in the "conspiracy trial" that followed the tumultuous 1968 Democratic Convention: (l. to. r.) Abbie Hoffman, John R. Froines, Lee Weiner, David Dellinger, Rennie Davis, and Tom Hayden. Jerry Rubin is seated.

Because of the elaborate precautions of city, state, and federal officials, the protesters had no way of getting close to the convention hall. Nevertheless, the police went on the attack as eagerly as if their quarry were trying to batter down the doors of the International Amphitheatre instead of being blocks away in the neighborhood of Grant Park and the Hilton Hotel. The frenzy even crept onto the convention floor where angered delegates, who had watched the events on television, were shouted down. Senator Abraham Ribicoff of Connecticut moved to the rostrum to nominate Senator McGovern and mentioned "the Gestapo on the streets of Chicago." He was yelled into momentary silence by a furious Mayor Daley and other Chicago politicians, allegedly to the accompaniment of insults and four-letter words.

The conventioneers and the other visitors left town, and Hubert Humphrey went on to defeat at the polls. Seven of those arrested were accused of "conspiracy" as the result of the violence. During the long, raucous trial before Federal Judge Julius Hoffman in 1970, Bobby Seales, one of the defendants, appeared in the courtroom bound and gagged after refusing to remain silent. In the end no one served time, even on Judge Hoffman's contempt rulings.

End of the Line: A report on the repeated confrontations between police and protesters during the convention prepared by Daniel Walker for the President's Commission on Violence used the term "police riot" and charged that on occasion "police discipline broke." Daley's image, and certainly his political influence outside of Chicago, were irreparably damaged, as he must have known. The city's reputation was further tattered in December 1969 by a predawn raid ordered by State's Attorney Edward Hanrahan on an apartment occupied by sleeping members of the Black Panther party. The nocturnal sortie, ostensibly to seize guns being hoarded by the Panthers, did find weapons. But it also resulted in the fatal shooting of two Panthers and the wounding of four others. Despite the raiders' lurid accounts of a firefight, a federal grand jury investigation showed that only one shot had come from a Panther bedroom in response to between 80 and 100 police bullets.

Things were never the same for Daley after the sixties. In 1972 two Illinois delegations went to the Democratic National Convention in Miami, but instead of Daley's group, the delegation headed by independent alderman William Singer was seated. In 1974 a close Daley associate was jailed on graft charges, and in the same year Daley gave indications of growing paranoia, perhaps stemming from his 1968 experiences. Faced with an operation, he chose his own time—a Sunday. City policemen were ordered to guard the hospital power plant against sabotage during the surgery. On December 20, 1976, Daley's 21-plus years as mayor of Chicago ended in his physician's office on the Magnificent Mile. Although he had suffered a stroke in 1974, his death took the city by surprise. He had seemed almost as permanent a fixture as Lake Michigan or the Water Tower.

A glittering portion of North Michigan Avenue above the river is lined with luxurious hotels and expensive shops. Chicago chauvinists call this "the Magnificent Mile."

The City Council named Michael Bilandic, alderman of the 11th Ward, as interim mayor. Bilandic easily won the general election in June 1978, having first defeated Alderman Roman Pucinski and a bright state senator named Harold Washington in the 1977 primary. The new mayor made few changes in the city's top administrative posts. Much as his idol, Daley, had done, he ran the city on an even keel. He seemed assured of obtaining his first four-year term when the next elections were held in 1979. But . . .

In 1977 Bilandic offered an unusual description of Daley: "He was not autocratic, he was not dictatorial. . . . I have become a better human being by having been touched by this bit of greatness."

The Snow Queen: One of Bilandic's key administrators, inherited from Daley, was Jane Byrne, commissioner of sales, weights, and measures. Shortly before Daley's death she also had been put in charge of public vehicle licenses. Byrne had moved up quickly in the Democratic organization, doing a fine job as consumer affairs commissioner and displaying a surprising knack for gaining newspaper attention. Eventually, to the poorly concealed annoyance of other members of the power structure, Daley made her his co-chairman of the Democratic Central Committee of Cook County (a post she quickly lost after his death).

At about the time Bilandic won the special election, negotiations were

Byrne, 43 years old, was a political protégé of Daley. She had been widowed in 1959 when her Marine pilot husband was killed near the Glenview Naval Air Station. On St. Patrick's Day, 1978, she married Jay McMullen, a former City Hall reporter for the Chicago Daily News.

Mirthful Jane: Former Mayor Jane Byrne, otherwise known (and photographed) as the Snow Queen.

underway between the two major taxicab companies and City Council representatives concerning a fare hike. Byrne began keeping a personal memo of what went on. The fare boost was granted in late July, and Byrne made no public protest. The information in her memo finally came out, however, through friendly reporters, and Byrne then went public, accusing Mayor Bilandic of "greasing" the increase. Bilandic denied the charge, and when he and Byrne each passed lie-detector tests in late November, he fired her.

Irked by the cold-shoulder treatment from those who had seemed friendly when Daley was alive—and still angry at having lost her job—Byrne announced in April that she was entering the 1979 mayoral primary. Few took her seriously, including Bilandic and the regular Democratic organization.

They failed to figure on the heavy snows that soon blanketed the town and the fact that there would be no third candidate to split the nonmachine and liberal vote. The storms brought more than 82 inches of snow during the winter, tying up auto traffic almost completely and causing mammoth delays on the overburdened bus and elevated lines. Garbage collections were also cut drastically. Byrne, meanwhile, was campaigning vigorously, and Chicagoans grew more and more sullen as Bilandic's snow-removal plans fizzled. Nevertheless, Byrne was not given even an outside chance, barring a miracle.

The miracle came in the form of a bright and sunny election day. Byrne's winter-weary supporters streamed to the polls in amazing numbers. Although the machine turned out its full quota of Bilandic votes (as it would have even in a blizzard), Byrne won her long-shot bet by about 17,000 votes.

Three's a Crowd: The new mayor provided the town with entertainment—some of it unintentional. She promoted parades and fireworks and fetes of various kinds. Byrne scattered promises lavishly, as if she were a Janey Appleseed: tax cuts, new city employees, and twice-weekly garbage collections. Her actions were often not only unpredictable, but also inexplicable. As her term neared an end, one inveterate Byrne-watcher summed up her administration as "management by hysteria."

This last service prompted State's Attorney Richard Daley—not known for his repartee—to say, "I expect . . . you'll soon to be able to open your door, toss your garbage out, and someone will be there to catch it."

Having prepared for reelection all along, Byrne had amassed more than $9 million for her war chest. The primary against State's Attorney Richard Daley, son of her late mentor, and Harold Washington (then a member of Congress) was the most expensive ever held in the city, with more than $12 million spent.

Although unopposed in the primary, Bernard Epton, the Republican candidate for mayor, was dismayed by the apathy of the press and his party's national officials. His understandable pique was increased when former governor Richard B. Ogilvie, a Republican, announced he was heading one of

Byrne's campaign committees. Epton could also hardly have been pleased at a newsman's offhand remark: "When Bernard Epton speaks, the television lights go off and the reporters put their pencils away."

A key issue during both the primary and general election campaigns was that Washington had been fined, had served 40 days in jail, and had been put on three years' probation for failure to file income tax returns in the sixties (although money had been withheld for taxes during those years). Washington freely admitted the charge, but pointed out that the total additional tax owed was $508.05.

Daley was endorsed by the *Chicago Sun-Times* and the *Chicago Tribune* but was disliked both by white racists and Byrne supporters, who feared he and Byrne would split enough votes to give Washington victory. A few days before the election, the racial issue was brought directly into the sunlight when Ogilvie asked his fellow Republicans to join him in voting for Byrne. Even more to the point, Alderman Edward ("Fast Eddie") Vrdolyak of the 10th Ward told a meeting of North Side political workers: "Don't kid yourself. . . . We're fighting to keep the city the way it is."

When the votes were tallied in the early hours of February 23, Washington had won the primary with 36 percent of the votes. Overwhelming support from black voters had combined with sufficient support from whites and the fact that the remaining white vote was split between Byrne and Daley.

All over town Democrats quickly became Republicans, most of them eager to see that a black did not become mayor of Chicago. While Daley had accepted defeat gracefully, Byrne went back on her pledge to support Washington against Epton. She announced she would be a write-in candidate since Washington would not be able to "preserve" the city if elected. When hoped-for support failed to materialize, Byrne soon announced she wouldn't be running after all.

Chicago's First Black Mayor: Washington and Epton (a wealthy attorney and war hero known as a generous giver to black causes) conducted a slam-bang, few-holds-barred campaign during which Washington's income tax and Epton's visits to psychiatrists were mentioned more than was necessary. While both candidates denounced the introduction of racism into the campaign, it kept being reintroduced.

Predictions that a Washington victory would cause the city to explode in racial conflict or at the least separate into two hostile camps proved groundless. No unusual racial friction followed Washington's April victory. But the City Council became divisive indeed. The largely white anti-Washington seg-

Victory smile: Chicago's first black mayor, Harold Washington.

ment—the 29 aldermen controlled by Vrdolyak and Edward Burke—seized the first council meeting after the election, grabbed the choice chairmanships, and did all they could to make the job of mayor unpalatable for Harold Washington. Washington was bloodied in the process, but he remained unbowed. He held to his campaign promise to remove politics from government—an impossible dream, but, then, the history of Chicago has been full of these.

Third City: It is now 150 years since Chicago's incorporation as a town—its sesquicentennial as a city comes in 1987. And it is 148 years since Judge Theophilus Smith was hooted down by a crowd of Chicagoans for the daft prediction that by the 1930s the city would boast a population of 100,000. "If we hadn't stopped you," one of them said, "you'd have made it a million." Many more than a million it was, and Judge Smith, a friend of growth, has been smiling in his grave for many years.

The area of Chicago is 228 square miles. The city has 3 airports, 12 major highways leading in, and a huge trucking industry. It also boasts 9 television stations, 31 radio stations, about 125 hospitals (some known internationally), and 95 colleges and universities, among them the University of Chicago, Northwestern, Columbia College, DePaul, Loyola, Roosevelt, the Circle Campus of the University of Illinois, and the Illinois Institute of Technology. The Art Institute, Adler Planetarium, Museum of Science and Industry, and Field Museum of Natural History are also world-renowned.

Both scholars and the public flock to the amazingly fine Chicago Historical Society, while the Newberry Library is one of the great research facilities for those interested in the history of this country and South America. There are also a number of ethnic and specialized museums, such as the Oriental Institute, and the public library's Cultural Center, on the edge of the Loop, has become a place of ideas and literary gatherings.

The theater is alive and doing very well with a wide-flung network of houses that spread from downtown across the neighborhoods and into the suburbs. The Chicago Symphony Orchestra has won international fame under Sir Georg Solti. Credit for the revival of opera in Chicago belongs largely to Carol Fox, who was instrumental in organizing the Lyric Opera more than a quarter of a century ago, following the collapse of the Chicago Opera Company.

Chicago has two major league baseball teams, the Cubs, owned for many years by the late Philip K. Wrigley and now by the *Chicago Tribune*, and the South Side White Sox, which twice have been the property of groups headed

by Bill Veeck, that delightful maverick, gadfly, conversationalist and—in recent years—designer of mobiles. Veeck and the Sox brought Chicago its last pennant, in 1959.

Then there are the Chicago Bears, founded and run for half a century by George Halas, who died in 1983, almost 70 years after being too late to board the doomed *Eastland;* the Chicago Bulls, Black Hawks, Blitz, and Sting; and—happily—the DePaul Blue Demons, perennial contenders for national basketball honors under the great Ray Meyer. Attention must be paid, too, to one of the finest concentrations of private and public golf courses to be found anywhere in the world.

Chicago has long been a literary center. The so-called Chicago Renaissance began shortly before the arrival of the twentieth century and vanished sometime in the 1920s, when many of its finest figures headed for New York or quit writing. Among early luminaries were Carl Sandburg; Theodore Dreiser; Frank Norris (whose novel *The Pit* dealt with the Board of Trade); Upton Sinclair (his *Jungle* spurred a federal investigation of conditions at the Chicago Stockyards); and Edna Ferber, George Ade, Sherwood Anderson, Finley Peter

Raconteur: Bill Veeck, baseball's superlative maverick, amusing sportscaster Al Lerner. No sports banquet (or extravaganza) is complete without him.

Winners: Gwendolyn Brooks was the first black writer to win a Pulitzer (*Annie Allen*, 1950); Saul Bellow's novels have won three National Book Awards and a Nobel; and Studs Terkel, interviewer supreme, is one of Chicago's best-loved (and best-selling) authors.

Dunne (*Mr. Dooley,*) Lew Sarrett, Edgar Lee Masters, Vachel Lindsay, Floyd Dell, and Maxwell Bodenheim.

Critic Vincent Starrett, who also wrote light verse and mysteries and was a world-class authority on Sherlock Holmes, remained in Chicago for 50 years or so until his death. Harry Hansen, Henry Blackman Sell, Francis Hackett, and Percy Hammond brightened the town for too short a time before going east, as did Ring Lardner and the *Chicago Tribune*'s Westbrook Pegler, a superb sportswriter turned acerbic right-winger.

Others who graced Chicago, at least for a while, included Richard Wright (*Native Son;*) Ben Hecht and Charles MacArthur (their comedy-drama *The Front Page* still delights audiences); James Farrell (*Studs Lonigan;*) Meyer Levin (*The Old Bunch;*) and one of the earliest proletarian writers, Jack Conroy (*The Disinherited.*) The late Thornton Wilder, winner of three Pulitzer Prizes for plays and novels, and Nelson Algren, author of many Chicago-based books, must be mentioned, along with the poet Gwendolyn Brooks and Saul Bellow, both still at their typewriters or word processors.

Frank London Brown, whose smile could warm a room, died young, but not before publishing *Trumbull Park,* the first novel describing (from personal experience) what happened when a black moved into a white and hostile Chicago neighborhood. Era Bell Thompson's *American Daughter* is a happier

A Short History of Chicago

factual account of a black girl growing up in the small town of Driscoll, North Dakota. It would be unthinkable not to also mention Fanny Butcher, the *Chicago Tribune*'s literary editor for half a century, or Claudia Cassidy of that paper, still one of the finest writers among music and drama critics anywhere.

Because this is a *short* history, we can only nod to such skilled Chicago craftsmen as James Park Sloan; Herman Kogan and Lloyd Wendt, a sometime team; Richard Stern, University of Chicago novelist; Cyrus Colter; Leon Forrest; Richard Dunlop; Bill Granger; Lerone Bennett, Jr.; Bill Brashler; Kenan Heise; Shel Silverstein—cartoonist, writer, and singer of sorts; Arthur Maling; Stuart Kaminsky; Eugene Kennedy; and the late Emmett Dedmon, whose *Fabulous Chicago* is one of the most engrossing books ever written about our town.

Like all major cities, Chicago has problems. Its potholes are almost as famous as Washington's cherry blossoms; windless summer days bring pollution alerts; and there are still charges of police brutality and corruption. Relationships between the city's diverse racial and national groups have improved, but the improvement isn't enough.

But potholes can be fixed. The transit system's finances no longer seem hopeless—there has even been talk of lower bus fares—and there are earnest efforts to better manage the infamous housing projects. A schedule has actually been posted for the collection of garbage, and recent tests indicate that public school students (with the help of improvements instituted by Supt. Ruth Love) are learning more than did the youngsters of a few years back. And the appointment of the city's first black police chief has boosted the black community's trust in its official protectors.

Black ghettoes remain, but it is no longer impossible to move out of them. A growing number of Chicagoans judge their fellow citizens by their minds and characters rather than by the color of their skins. Most residents consider their town an excellent place to live, and indeed few cities can match Chicago's natural advantages: Lake Michigan (both a superb air-conditioning device and a waterway to countless destinations) and the central location that made the city a national rail center and possessor of the world's busiest airport.

Chicago's unofficial slogan is "I Will!" This is perhaps the midwestern version of the old British family motto, "Press On, Regardless!"—which Chicagoans did after the Fort Dearborn massacre, the Great Fire, and the plague of gangsters half a century ago. May they continue to do so.

Sears Tower: The world's tallest building is in mid-town Chicago, and rises 1,454 ft. above street level.

Selected Bibliography

Addams, Jane. *Twenty Years at Hull House*. New York: Macmillan, 1910.

Andreas, Alfred Theodore. *History of Chicago, from the Earliest Period to the Present*. Chicago: A.T. Andreas, 1884–1886. Three volumes. Absorbing account of Chicago's beginnings, with much source material.

Andrews, Wayne. *Battle for Chicago*. New York: Harcourt, Brace, 1946.

Angle, Paul, editor. *Prairie State. Impressions of Illinois, 1673–1967, by Travellers and Other Observers*. Chicago and London: University of Chicago Press, 1968. An absorbing potpourri.

————. *The Great Chicago Fire*. Chicago: Chicago Historical Society, 1971. Accounts by eight survivors of the Great Fire. New edition.

Cromie, Robert. *The Great Chicago Fire*. New York: McGraw-Hill, 1958. Chronological account of the conflagration.

Cromie, Robert, with Joseph Pinkston. *Dillinger, a Short and Violent Life*. New York: McGraw-Hill, 1962. Story of the Indiana farm-boy who died in a Chicago alley.

Dedmon, Emmett. *Fabulous Chicago, a Great City's History and People* (enlarged edition). New York: Atheneum, 1981. An engrossing social history.

Farr, Finis. *Chicago: A Personal History of America's Most American City*. New Rochelle, N.Y.: Arlington House, 1973.

Fitzgerald, Kathleen. *Brass: Jane Byrne and the Pursuit of Power*. Chicago: Contemporary, 1981.

Flinn, John J. *Official Guide to the World's Columbian Exposition in the City of Chicago. State of Illinois, May 1 to October 26, 1893, by Authority of the United States of America, Containing a Brief Historical Review of American Development, An Account of Legislation Relating to the Exposition, Its Form of Organization and Government and Full Information Respecting All Features of the Exposition, Including Classification of Departments, the Grounds and Main Buildings, the State and Foreign Buildings and Pavilions, the Notable Exhibits, Etc., Etc.,* Chicago: The Columbian Guide Co., 1893.

Granger, Bill and Lori. *Fighting Jane: Mayor Jane Byrne and the Chicago Machine.* New York: Dial, 1980.

Halper, Albert, editor. *This is Chicago: An Anthology.* New York: Henry Holt, 1952.

Harrison, Carter. *Stormy Years: The Autobiography of Carter H. Harrison.* Indianapolis and New York: Bobbs Merrill, 1935.

Kaufman, Mervyn. *Father of Skyscrapers, a Biography of Louis Sullivan.* Boston and Toronto: Little, Brown, 1969.

Kirkland, Joseph. *The Story of Chicago.* Chicago: Dibble, 1892.

Kebabian, John S. *The Haymarket Affair and the Trial of the Chicago Anarchists 1886.* New York: H.P. Kraus, 1970. Collection of original manuscripts, letters, articles, etc.

Kobler, John. *Capone: The Life and World of Al Capone.* New York: Putnam, 1971.

Kogan, Herman and Cromie, Robert. *The Great Fire, Chicago, 1871.* New York: Putnam, 1971. Photos and text on the famous fire.

Kogan, Herman and Rick. *Yesterday's Chicago.* Miami: E.A. Seeman, 1976. Text and numerous photographs.

Kogan, Herman and Wendt, Lloyd. *Chicago, a Pictorial History.* New York: Dutton, 1958.

Lewis, Lloyd and Smith, Henry Justin. *Chicago, the History of Its Reputation.* New York: Harcourt, Brace, 1929.

Lieberman, Archie, and Cromie, Robert. *Chicago.* Superb photos by Lieberman with accompanying text.

Lowe, David, editor. *The Great Chicago Fire in Eyewitness Accounts and 70 Contemporary Photographs and Illustrations.* New York: Dover, 1979. Paperback.

Masters, Edgar Lee. *The Tale of Chicago*. New York: Putnam, 1933.

Mayer, Harold M. and Wade, Richard C. *Chicago: Growth of a Metropolis*. Chicago and London: University of Chicago Press, 1969. Invaluable record.

McIlvaine, Mabel. *Reminiscences of Chicago During the Civil War*. New York: Citadel, 1967.

McPhaul, John J. *Deadlines and Monkeyshines, the Fabled World of Chicago Journalism*. Englewood Cliffs, N.J.: Prentice-Hall, 1962.

Moore, William T. *Dateline Chicago: A Veteran Newsman Recalls Its Heydey*. New York: Taplinger, 1973.

O'Conner, Len. *Clout: Mayor Daley and His City*. Chicago: Regnery, 1975.

————. *Requiem: The Decline and Demise of Mayor Daley and His Era*. Chicago: Contemporary Books, 1977.

Pasley, Fred D. *Al Capone: The Biography of a Self-Made Man*. New York: Ives Washburn, 1930.

Pierce, Bessie Louise. *A History of Chicago* (1673–1897). Three volumes. New York: Knopf, 1937, 1940, 1957. Superb complement to Andreas.

Rakove, Milton L. *Don't Make No Waves, Don't Back No Losers; An Insider's Analysis of the Daley Machine*. Bloomington: Indiana University Press, 1975.

————. *We Don't Want Nobody Sent; an Oral History of the Daley Years*. Bloomington: University of Indiana Press, 1979.

Royko, Mike. *Boss: Richard J. Daley and His Era*. Chicago: Dutton, 1971.

Sandburg, Carl. *The Chicago Race Riots, July 1919*. New York: Harcourt, Brace and World, 1969. With added preface material by Ralph McGill (first published in 1919).

Sheahan, Joseph W. and Upton, George P. *The Great Conflagration; Chicago Its Past, Present and Future*. Chicago, Philadelphia, Cincinnati: Union Publishing Co., 1871. (Title incomplete—actually continues 71 additional words.)

Smith, Alson Jesse. *Chicago's Left Bank*. Chicago: Regnery, 1953.

Smith, Henry Justin. *Chicago: A Portrait*. New York and London: Century, 1931.

————. *Chicago's Great Century, 1833–1933*. Chicago: Consolidated, 1933.

Trollope, Anthony. *North America*, edited, with an introduction, notes, and new materials, by Donald Smalley and Bradford Allen Booth. New York: Knopf, 1951.

Wagenknecht, Edward. *Chicago*. Norman: University of Oklahoma Press, 1964.

Wendt, Lloyd. *Chicago Tribune: The Rise of a Great American Newspaper*. Chicago: Rand McNally, 1979. Masterful and engrossing work by a former *Tribune* editor.

Wendt, Lloyd and Kogan, Herman. *Big Bill of Chicago*. Indianapolis and New York: Bobbs-Merrill, 1953.

————. *Give the Lady What She Wants*. Chicago, New York, San Francisco: Rand McNally, 1952. A lively history of Marshall Field's.

————. *Lords of the Levee*. Indianapolis and New York, 1943. All about Hinky-Dink and The Bath.

Wentworth, John and others. *Early Chicago History*. Chicago: Fergus, 1876.

Also: Back copies of Chicago newspapers including the *Tribune, Sun-Times* and *Daily News,* and articles from various sources including the *Journal of the Illinois State Historical Society, Harper's, Atlantic Monthly, Lakeside Monthly, Century,* and *Cosmopolitan.*

PICTURE CREDITS

Andreas: 6, 8, 12, 14, 15, 21, 26, 32, 33, 34, 35, 36, 42, 44, 46, 49, 50, 52, 54, 56–57, 58, 65, 66, 67, 68, 69, 70, 71, 78, 80, 82, 86, 89, 96, 98

Chicago Bears: 114

Chicago Public Library: 128

Chicago Tribune: 120

Commission on Chicago Historical and Architectural Landmarks: 99, 102

The Contemporary Forum: 132

Robert Cromie: 76, 78, 92, 94, 104, 106, 112

Fox, Cole, 63

Historic New Orleans Collection: 10

Jesse Jackson for President Committee: 124

Kirkland: 18, 20, 23, 24, 30, 37

Kogan Collection: 9, 108, 111, 113, 115, 117, 118, 126

The Library of Congress: 60, 116

Mayor's Office: 129

Hy Roth: 122

Sears, Roebuck, and Co.: 133

Joan Shaffer: 132

Sheehan and Upton: *The Great Conflagration*: 87

University of Chicago: 132

University of Illinois at Chicago, The Library Jane Addams Collection: 103

University of Illinois at Chicago, The Library Manuscript Collection: 100

Mary Frances Veeck: 131

Index

Note: Page numbers in italics refer to photographs and maps.